Brough Superior

The Rolls-Royce
of Motorcycles

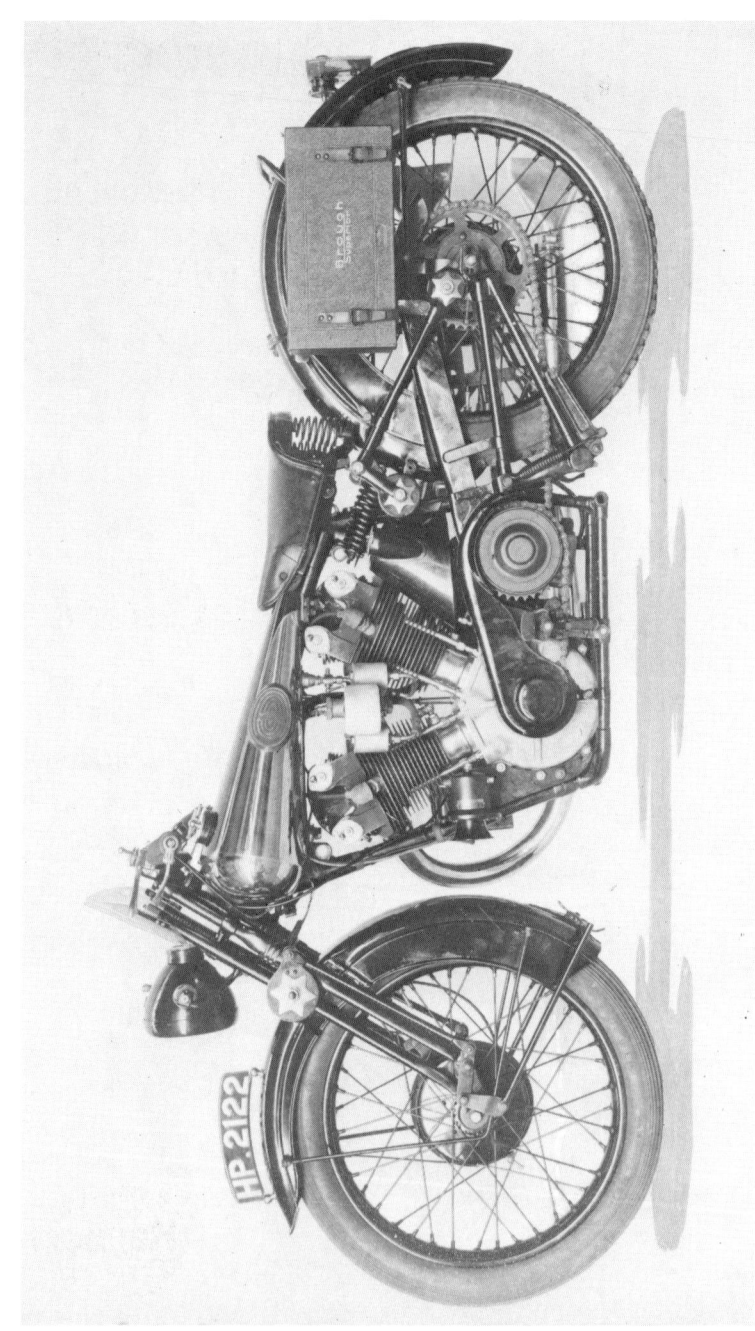

The beautiful spring frame SS100

Brough Superior

The Rolls-Royce of Motorcycles

Ronald H. Clark

First published by Goose & Son in 1964
Second edition published in 1974
Third edition published by G. T. Foulis & Company in 1984
Reprinted by Haynes Publishing in 1998

British Library Cataloguing-in-Publication Data:
A catalogue record for this book
is available from the British Library

ISBN 1 85960 438 2

Library of Congress catalog card No. 84-048788

Haynes Publishing, Sparkford,
Nr Yeovil, Somerset, BA22 7JJ

Tel. 01963 440635 Fax: 01963 440001
Int. tel: +44 1963 440635 Fax: +44 1963 440001

E-mail: sales@haynes-manuals.co.uk
Web site: http://www.haynes.com

Haynes North America Inc.
861 Lawrence Drive, Newbury Park,
California 91320 USA

Printed in Great Britain

The List of Acknowledgements

E. N. Adlington, Esq., Elstree
Messrs Barr & Stroud Ltd, Anniesland, Glasgow
R. Berry, Esq., Manchester
George Brough, Esq., Redhill, Nottinghamshire
Brough Superior Club
C. E. Burgess, Esq., Tottenham
J. H. Carr, Esq., Addingham
T. Eccles, Esq., Burnley
G. M. Fitzpatrick, Esq., Arlesey
W. S. Gibbard, Esq., Sewardstonebury
S. M. Greening, Esq., Winchmore Hill
Harold Karslake, the late, and Mrs Karslake, Kettering
C. G. Leppard, Esq., Cheam
Sir William Lyons, Coventry
C. Mathews, Esq., Plumstead
J. N. Mavrogordato, Esq., Salisbury
C. Mortimer, Esq., Weybridge
Motor Cycle, The, editor and staff, and for permission to use the illus-
    trations taken from that journal
Motor Cycling, editor and staff, and for permission to use the illustrations
    taken from that journal also
Motosacoche à Genève, Gèneva
E. S. Prestwich, Esq., Chalfont St Giles
Messrs J. A. Prestwich & Co. Ltd, Tottenham
A. R. J. Ramsey, Esq., Hinchley Wood, for help with patents
B. Robinson, Esq., Newthorpe
L. E. Shelley, Esq., East Sheen
Mrs V. D. Spencer (*née* Baragwanath), Kentish Town
R. W. Storey, Esq., Basford
D. Webb, Esq., the late, Bulwell
I. J. Webb, Esq., Basford
Stanley Whysall, Esq., Bulwell

The List of Works Consulted

Autocar, The
Messrs Barr & Stroud Ltd, engine catalogues
British Legion *Journal*
Brough Superior catalogues, all editions
Brough Superior Club, Newsletters
Engineering
English Mechanic
Matchless Motor Cycles, handbooks
Motorall, Das
Motor, The
Motor Cycle, The
Motor Cycle & Cycle Trader, The
Motor Cycling
Motor Cycling News
Motor Cyclist Review
Motorist & Wheelman, The
Motosacoche à Genève, engine catalogues
Nottingham Evening News
Patent Specifications, various
Messrs J. A. Prestwich & Co. Ltd, engine catalogues and published
    literature
Vintage & Veteran

Contents

Foreword to the First Edition

Mr Clark must have gone to a tremendous amount of trouble and literally given years of time to collate all the information he has gathered and put together in this history of the Brough Superior.

I am honoured that he should ask me to write this foreword and I congratulate him on the accuracy of the hundreds of details he has gathered together by sheer enthusiasm and love of the thing he is writing about. Such a man makes me feel very humble and grateful.

I can just—only just—remember the time when I didn't ride a motor-bike! I should be ten years old—or perhaps less when my father took a contraption called a front-drive Werner in exchange for a debt. This wonderful machine which I realised I might one day ride without having to pedal it (I couldn't reach the pedals anyway) had the engine hung in front of the steering head immediately below the handlebars and drove the front wheel via a flat leather belt about one inch wide. It had an incandescent tube for ignition and the front portion of the petrol tank was a separate compartment containing a thick pad of cotton wool which was fed from the main tank by a tap. When you saturated the pad—not too much and not too little—you supplied the petrol–air ratio through a revolving sleeve on the right-hand-side handlebar grip—that was called a wick carburettor. My father and my elder brother suspended the front wheel about six inches from the floor securely fastened in a specially made stand. Mother supplied the mat for Father and, when he was tired, my brother to kneel on. For hours and hours, night after night, these two brave men pulled and pulled the engine over compression whilst Mother and I held on to the back portion of the bike in case it *did* start. And that is what did happen about the fifth night, when by much trial and error Father found the right petrol–air ratio—and the right heat for the ignition tube.

When Father left that bike with everything recorded about how to start it *on the road* next time, he little thought that a wee small boy was waiting for him to close his bedroom door, go downstairs, remove the belt and his shoes, push the bike away from the works in the dead of the night—and in dead silence wait for the dawn. That was the hour when perhaps the B.S. foundation stone was laid.

I set things just as they were the previous night when as the novel writers say 'The Engine burst into Life'. I pushed, and I pushed and I pushed with what was called 'the compression tap' open but the 'bursting into life' didn't happen again until I had pushed about three miles, all the time trying different positions of the air slide on the right-hand grip. All at once a thin flame shot out of the open compression tap—a mighty leap *on* to the saddle (you didn't sit *in* 'em in those days) and we were AWAY—we were motoring—Dennis May's 'Basford Bahnstormer' was born! That was the start, and it set something alight inside me which I thank God is still burning.

A lot of water has gone under Trent Bridge since that never-to-be-forgotten dawn, but from the time that Werner shot its first flame through the compression tap to the last time I twisted the throttle grip of an SS100 yesterday, no man has enjoyed a fuller and more pleasurable life.

I have been blessed with a wonderful father and mother who gave me a healthy body and who literally worked like Trojans the whole of their lifetime so as to make it possible for me to carry on where they left off remembering their slogan—'Try to make it better'.

For forty-seven years I have had a wife who has helped in every way, and oh, so very understanding! Early B.S. lads will know what I mean.

I have always had, and still have, a wonderful staff of loyal men and women, the name 'Brough Superior' meaning just the same to them that it means to me.

I am proud and grateful to the large number of grand lads who rode my productions in Trials, Races and Hill climbs and have made their names famous throughout the world.

George Brough

Foreword to the Third Edition

12 Private Road
SHERWOOD
Nottingham.

I am so proud that this "History of the Brough Superior" has reached another edition.

Mr. Clark must have a deep feeling of satisfaction after all his effort in producing such a very fine book – and how happy George would have been to know of this – and of the lasting popularity and appreciation of his motor cycles after so many years. Reading it again brings to me memories of all the thrills and excitement of those days. Never a week went by without some motor cyclist joining us for lunch at *Pendine* from the greatest to the least well known. From the age of twenty they were my life!

George and his motor cycles have given and are still giving pleasure to many people. Sometimes I think he will never really die.

God bless him.

E. Constance Brough

The Introductory Remarks

Looking back over the years one finds the English motor-cycle immediately after the First World War was in a similar undeveloped state to that of the English steam locomotive at the time of the Rainhill Trials in 1829. One can safely say that what the development of the steam locomotive owes to George Stephenson, the development of the English motor-cycle owes to George Brough. In 1919 the English motor-cycle was generally rather a crude piece of work, with narrow beaded-edge tyres, no rear springing, poor forks, gas lighting and temperamental electrical components. Preponderating was the ill-balanced single-cylinder engine with a clout on the front chain or belt every 720° of crankshaft revolution—as is so often the case even today.

On the following pages I have endeavoured to show the results of an original mind applied to the English motor-cycle. How, for example, the home-produced big vee engine was improved, often to meet George Brough's demands, until the New World's stranglehold on racing and private sales was broken. Now, unfortunately, the wheel has turned full circle and a customer today requiring a vee twin has to buy a New World product! The home country, apparently resting on its pre-war oars, has lost the skill to make them as it lacks the skill to compete in the two-stroke field with the Far East. Again, in the era of the Brough Superior the customer was always right, and if he wanted a vee engine he could get one. Today we are fobbed off with a vertical double single of poor balance, and if one argues the result—usually—is a crude term from the agent. I gather the industry is now somewhat ashamed it ever made vee engines!

Also on the following pages I hope I have given enlightenment to some on what a fine piece of design and engineering the motor-cycle can be. By some, I mean the ignorant requiring a wheel at each corner and those prejudiced against motor-cycles in general, and ignorant of the Brough Superior in particular. Those to whom the motor-cycle, including the Brough Superior, has no snob value and who, with an insolent stare, usually display their ignorance like a coat of arms.

The Brough Superior was really a remarkable achievement and practically a one-man concern. George Brough had not only a flair for incorporating 'lines' in a machine, and the organising ability to get it built, but a happy knack of attracting and keeping the right kind of loyal staff to help him. He knew, too, the valuable help and ideas users of the Brough Superior could provide. Hints and data by many of the racing and trials men were used to perfect details in subsequent models. This was one small way in which he always strove to improve the product. Another way is indicated by the variety of engines and machines—unorthodox judged by diehard single-cylinder standards —which after strenuous testing became available to the public.

This high standard of perfection of design and detail was naturally costly. Today, with rigidity of detail imposed by multiple mass production, especially of components, the Brough Superior produced to pre-war standards of quality and excellence would be prohibitive in cost, and so it never appeared on the post-war market.

It was built to an ideal and appreciated and purchased by connoisseurs. Many were somewhat impecunious, but a Brough was worth saving for and so save they did, the author amongst them. Therefore the young man of yesterday treasured his Brough Superior once he had it, maintained it and handled it with the appropriate skills. Today, with high wages so easily obtained, ownership of a fast machine is that much easier and few graduate the hard way from a tenth-hand to a new one, thus learning much. Consequently there is now apt to be a lack of skill and consideration for others on the road.

One must remember too that the make was produced over a period of twenty-one years forming the golden age of motor-cycling. It was an age accentuated by the exploits of great men on great machines, some of whom receive honourable mention on later pages. It was a period when motor-cycles looked like motor-cycles, when decent English was used when writing about them, and when there was great pride of possession. It was yet another era that is past, years moreover the like of which we shall never see again.

Not infrequently we hear how vastly superior the present-day machine is compared with its pre-war predecessors. Is it? The only fair basis of comparison is brake horse-power per 100 c.c. of swept volume at ordinary revolutions per minute. The later 1,000 c.c. J.A.P. for road use produced 7·4 b.h.p. per 100 c.c. and an average of several post-war engines of 49, 248 and 598 c.c. respectively produce 5·75 b.h.p. per 100 c.c.! In the case of the smallest it has to peak at 2,000 r.p.m. more than the big vee. I need say no more!

In normal road trim the Brough Superior was renowned for its quietness, a virtue sadly lacking in present-day machines and a main cause of public antipathy to motor-cycling. Therefore today's manufacturer is partly to blame for riders of my generation being looked at askance by many who, under other circumstances, would behave normally. These antipathetics must remember that the average motor-cycle requires eighteen square feet of road and the average motor car one hundred and ten, and extended use of single-track vehicles would logically therefore reduce congestion. Thus a statutory limit of six million motor-cycles and four million cars, with proof of need to acquire a licence, would solve the problem of our roads. Admittedly not very flattering with the motor-car usually regarded as a status symbol—but it would arrest the filching of good agricultural land, conserve the amenities of the countryside and facilitate the preservation of our building inheritance.

Although the last Rolls Royce of Motor-Cycles left the works in 1940, the make is far from dead, as evidenced by the Brough Superior Club, founded in 1958 and now embracing a membership of over two hundred. Should any reader require particulars of the club I should be pleased to forward them; as, I trust, readers will appraise me of any interesting Brough they may discover.

Naturally the size of this volume has had to be kept within reasonable bounds, and therefore it has been impossible to include every success gained by this famous make, every small detail and modification at times incorporated in the machines sold to the public, and details of all the great bicycles which have helped to make Brough history. But the reader will find all the essentials and, I hope, much information which is new to him. Moreover, it is with no little pride I own to having covered over a quarter of a million miles on Brough Superiors; in fact, all the information used in my previous books on the steam engine was collected by this means and the bicycle became known at more than one works up and down the country. I am still an active rider. This last fact I feel to be a vital and necessary qualification when writing on the subject.

So many kind people have helped with various data that I have included a list of acknowledgements, and if I have omitted anyone it is quite unintentional. I am not so sanguine as to imagine there are no mistakes, they will creep in however careful all may be, so I would appreciate any errors being pointed out. I cannot conclude without offering special thanks to the staff at the works and of the motor-cycling journals, all of whom have been most helpful. Then there is the maker who, not being content with giving me every support and writing the Foreword, checked through the whole of the text, a task shared too by Mrs Brough with her characteristic understanding.

Lastly I would like to thank John Moore of Goose & Son Ltd, who has undertaken to publish the first book dealing solely with one make of English motor-cycle.

RONALD H. CLARK

Introduction to the 1998 reprint

I feel it is a rare experience to have to write an introduction to the fourth printing of one of my several books. That books are published in editions subsequent to the first is not unusual but a fourth, with a third publisher, must be less common. For the author, like me who has passed his 93rd birthday, it makes the occasion practically unique. It also confirms that motorcycling all the year round keeps one fit!

That there have been few alterations or corrections needed is another source of pride and pleasure, and my thanks are due to those Brough riders and owners who have contacted me with additional items of history, mechanics and general Brough lore.

I can only hope that this volume will be received with a similar reception to that bestowed upon the others. Then, the effort devoted to its conception will have made the venture so worthwhile. One must not omit to remember the great part played by Haynes Publishing who showed great enterprise in its production.

RONALD H. CLARK
Norwich

Publisher's notice:

Because the original paste-up and film for this book had been lost or destroyed before we acquired the option to publish this third edition, we have had to resort to photographic reproduction from a copy of the second reprint. Whilst we have tried our best to obtain good reproduction, we apologise for any imperfections we have been unable to correct.

CHAPTER I

The Early Days

Often in the history of engineering and technology we find a situation or set of circumstances propitious for the inspiration or establishment of a certain project. The necessity of draining mines in the late seventeenth and early in the eighteenth centuries stimulated the development of the steam engine for pumping, and again, the increase of mechanically propelled road transport after the Heavy Motor Car Orders of 1903 hastened some improvements in all types of vehicles and roads. There are many other examples, including the inception of the Brough Superior.

In 1861 William Edward Brough was born at Clay Cross, Derbyshire, and we first hear of him as mechanic in charge of the large steam winding engine at Cinderhill Colliery belonging to the Babington Colliery Company, in the directorship then of Sir Charles Seely. At this period electricity too was fast becoming of commercial importance in its various applications, so it is not surprising after a few years to find W. E. Brough, a man of no little initiative, foreman electrician to the colliery, a post he held until he left in 1899.

During his tenure of office at Cinderhill he built 10 Mandalay Street, Basford in 1889 and resided there until 1895 when he moved to Vernon Road, still in Basford, and built there a small works with residential quarters attached, the plot being close to the railway and on the south side of it. The object of the works? Newfangled motor-cars and motor-cycles were 'coming in' at this period and W. E. Brough was far-sighted enough to see the great possibilities in this direction. One must remember a training in steam engineering and steam plant and similar machinery is a great asset to any man, and as in the later case of W. O. Bentley and many others, proved to be so in this instance.

In 1898–9 he completed a small car powered by a $3\frac{1}{2}$ h.p. De Dion engine with a final belt drive. A second car, made in 1908, is to be seen in Fig. 1. A smaller $2\frac{1}{2}$ h.p. De Dion engine powered a motor-tricycle just before 1899. W. E. Brough's first motor-cycle, 'All Brough' shall we say, appeared in 1902 utilising a small engine with

1　*William Brough's second motor-car*

fixed belt drive seen in Fig. 2. Note the curious engine position ahead
of and below the bottom bracket and the pedalling gear for l.p.a.
(light pedal assistance). In addition bicycles, petrol tanks and
similar accessories were turned out for his own requirements and
for the now growing industry generally. Like many pioneers of this
period, W. E. Brough was graced with an inventor's mind, and an
early galvanometer originated by him is yet preserved at the works.

In those days let us remember that young men were not tenderly
spoiled by so-called welfare, but this W. E. Brough minded not a bit,
and by his own efforts he attended evening classes in Nottingham on
engineering subjects and often walked there and back if no other
transport was available. He was proud of his physical strength in
addition, and one of his employees testifies to William's ability to
wield a 14 lb. hammer and swing it at any angle. My informant added
he felt quite safe holding the tool to be struck in his hand! A caulking
hammer, probably one of the first tools he ever bought when starting
out in life, both head and shaft now polished, is still treasured by
George and shown to kindred spirits with no little pride. Such was the

atmosphere of motor and motor-cycle engineering in which William's family of two sons was tutored and reared.

On 18 June 1885 was born W. E. Brough's elder son called also William Edward after his father. George was the second son, being born at 10 Mandalay Street on 21 April 1890.

From an early age both sons naturally, one could almost say automatically, became actively involved in motor-cycling. Thus we find William junior entering his first trial, the A.C.C. End to End in 1906, winning a gold medal, his number being 23. George was number 24, both on 'Broughs' of course, and William's certificate remained displayed in the proprietor's office for many years. George finished three days behind the last man and had to apply l.p.a. everywhere except downhill!

Besides the car in 1908 the motor-cycle was now improved to the extent seen in Fig. 3 where the engine is now in the accepted place,

2   First 'All Brough' motor-cycle of 1902

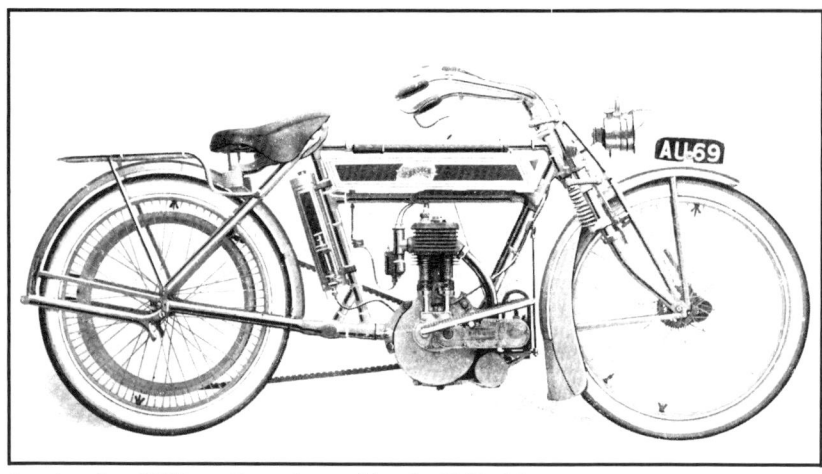

3 Another William Brough machine in 1908–10

vertical, larger, more robust and enjoying the old rating of 3½ h.p. George incidentally is in the driver's seat in Fig. 1 and on the saddle of the bicycle in Fig. 2. In 1909 William junior, however, transferred his energies to shipbuilding, but returned to his father's works in 1921 and remained until 1923, after which he took no further part in the firm's activities.

Not so George, whom we find remaining with his father and testing machines as they were completed, including some experimental jobs, one in particular having a single cylinder and combined rotary- and sleeve-valve, a design very much ahead of its time—the engine in its frame is to be seen in Fig. 4. Note the plug in the side of the head, the sleeve being so turned that the plug points were only uncovered at the moment of firing, thus preventing fouling of the points to a very great extent. Another Brough engine rated at 2½ h.p. had automatic inlet valves, but in the Nottingham Road Trials in 1911 George rode a vee twin produced in the Vernon Road Works, and Fig. 5 shows the ingenious arrangement of the timing gear with the cover removed. From Fig. 6 can be gleaned the general lines of the complete machine, its excellent finish and contemporary sidecar replete with decorated wickerwork. Once again George is in the saddle exercising great care as the passenger is his mother.

One of George's greatest feats during this period was to come first in the London–Edinburgh Trial three consecutive years—1910, 1911 and 1912. This won for him the *Motor Cycling* Cup, one of the

above: 4   William Brough's rotary- and sleeve-valve engine

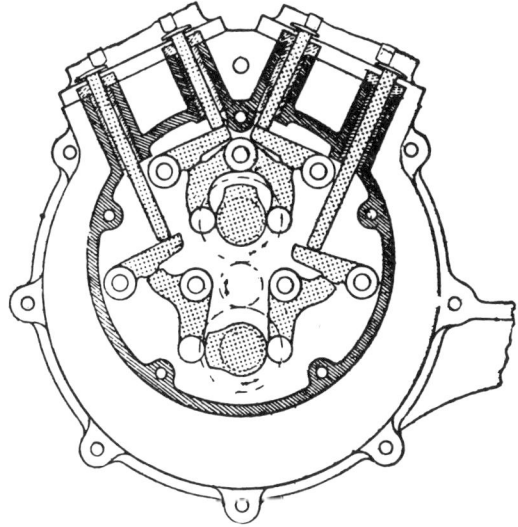

5   Timing gear of the 1911 vee twin Brough engine

Note the rear exhaust cam follower has been drawn bearing on the lobe of the cam, in which case the exhaust valve should have been shown in the fully open position.

6   George Brough with his mother as passenger in 1911

finest I have ever seen, which has a permanent resting place in the drawing room at Pendine.

Flat or horizontally opposed twins were conceived and produced in 1911 and so we find the 1913 Senior T.T. machine ridden by George sporting an engine of this form. W. E. Brough called these machines the Model G—G for George!

For 1921 a new model appeared having a horizontally opposed twin engine with cylinders $70 \times 64\frac{1}{2}$ mm. totalling 496 c.c. All of the machine with the exception of gearbox, chains, tyres and saddle, etc., was made at Vernon Road, including even the necessary castings. Two unusual features were the cylinders and gearbox fixing. The cylinders were made in three parts, the barrel, the head and the two separate ports bolted on to the head at an included angle of 60°. The Sturmey-Archer gearbox was mated to the underside of the crankcase on a planed mounting so that chain tension was varied by sliding the box to suit—practically unit construction. Pushrods for operating the overhead valves were arranged along the tops of the cylinders to be seen in the illustration in Fig. 7.

A larger 6 h.p. machine of 692 c.c. was also available which together with the 496 c.c. version remained in production until manufacture of the Brough ceased in 1925. Of these flat twins W. E. Brough & Co. said: 'The fittings, additional to those which are produced in the Works, are all of high-class manufacture, produced by firms whose names are famous throughout the motor-cycling world.' Perhaps their best testimonial was to enter seven machines in the London–Edinburgh Trial in 1920 and to win six gold and one silver medals!

In common with every English engineering concern of any standing the Vernon Road Works during the First World War was most actively

7   *William Brough's fast flat twin of 496 c.c.*

engaged in essential production for the Admiralty, petrol-priming installations for Rolls Royce aero engines and 13-pounder A.A. shells. Naturally such effort curtailed development and manufacture of motor-cycles.

In addition to running the Basford Works successfully, W. E. Brough was quick to patent any good idea his fertile mind produced, and a list of his eleven patents, ranging from fittings for cycles to improvements in internal combustion engine valves, will be found in the appropriate appendix.

Such then was the background and atmosphere in which George Brough grew up, most favourable and encouraging for one with ideas of improving the English motor-cycle.

CHAPTER II

The First Brough Superiors

During the First World War George Brough spent part of this period with Messrs White & Poppe of Coventry working on the development of aero and similar engines and at the same time, his limited leisure permitting, designed a new flat twin motor-cycle, parts of which were actually made at Vernon Road. The end of this war found him in partnership with his father, a situation he thought most favourable for developing his dreams of producing a luxury machine of large capacity, excellently made and finished to appeal to the connoisseur. But father William looked askance at such a serious venture, whereupon George, undaunted and younger in outlook, and with the poet's dictum 'nothing venture, nothing win' clearly before him, touched his father for his one-third share in the Basford business telling him too he would make a Brough, superior to the average motor-cycle then procurable, and immediately bought a small plot of land in Haydn Road, Nottingham, and erected thereon a small workshop, office and stores.

For a few weeks between seceding from his father's works and settling in at Haydn Road, the first four or five machines were built late in 1919 in the small garage opposite the Lodge of Stockhill House, which had been built previously by his father. Directly the new but small premises were ready the Lodge garage was vacated and *Brough Superiors* began to emerge gaily to lucky customers whilst *Brufsup, Nottingham* became a new telegraphic interest via Imperial Cables to be memorised like the postal address *Haydn Road*, by countless big twin enthusiasts.

Proper production commenced in the new home early in 1920, although some items such as frames and other accessories were made out in Coventry and Birmingham, and engines from Tottenham and Geneva were produced to the young maker's designs.

Let us now enjoy Fig. 8 depicting the Mark I Brough Superior of 1919–20 powered by an engine specially manufactured by J. A. Prestwich Ltd, having cylinders $90 \times 77 \cdot 5$ mm. and affectionately known by many of my generation as the '90 Bore'. The silent alchemy

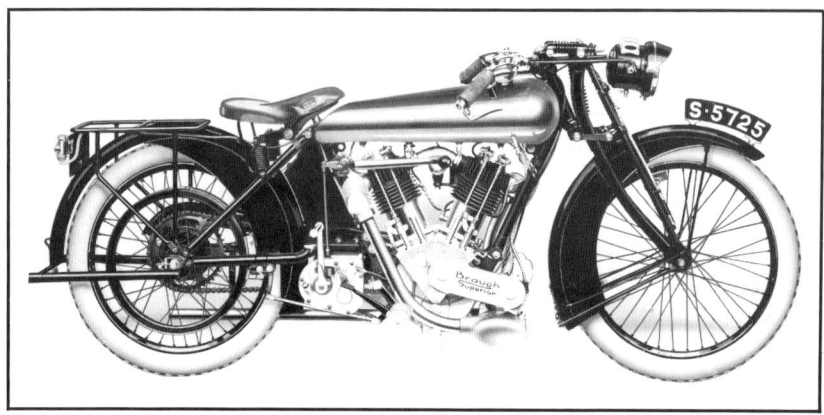

8 *The first Brough Superior of 1919*

of forty years dims not the mind in recollection of the mellow murmur with which these big engines turned. 'Twould interrupt a happy train of thought in many minds no doubt to state the specification later on in an appendix, so here it is to hand:

Engine Specially manufactured for the Brough Superior by Messrs J. A. Prestwich, 50° V Twin, 90 mm. bore × 77·5 mm. stroke, overhead valves of special alloy steel, roller bearing big ends, and on main shaft, aluminium alloy pistons. The lower portion of the cylinders are heavily plated, preventing rust and facilitating cleaning. All the overhead valve gear is plated, and the crankcase is sand-blast finished. The exhaust arrangements are neatly and cleverly carried out, attached to the overhead ports are two finned aluminium heat dissipating ports leading the exhaust gases into correctly streamlined exhaust pipes, thence into a large cast aluminium silencer, and out through a perfectly straight extension pipe to the rear of machine. The carburettor is attached to a specially designed aluminium casting forming the induction pipe. The contour of this casting and of the silencer and the bulbous nose of the tank are harmonious.

Three Speed Gear This is made by the Sturmey-Archer Gear Co. and is an exclusive production for the Brough Superior. A shock-absorber is self-contained in the clutch body, and all the wheels and shafts have been stiffened up to withstand the tremendous power available. The gear ratios are 3·25 (top), 5·2 (second), and 8·2 (bottom). Special ratios can be fitted for particular purposes. The introduction of a shock-absorber in the gearbox provides a beautifully sweet drive.

Carburettor A special type of multiple jet A.M.A.C. two-lever instrument is fitted as standard. Opinions on carburation are divided, and the maker is willing to fit any other make of instrument to order.

Ignition M.L. magneto, with handlebar control. The contact-breaker return spring is very neatly housed, so as to obviate the usual unsightly external spring. The magnets are heavily plated. When dynamo lighting is fitted, a Lucas Magdyno is supplied.

Frame Exceptionally strong, and will stand any amount of abuse and misuse. All lugs are scientifically designed to adopt a straight tube frame and to house the respective units without the slightest amount of room being wasted. This point will be particularly noticeable from the illustration. Sidecar attachment lugs are arranged in the construction, and only double-butted tubes are used. All lugs for attaching tank, toolbag, etc., are brazed on part and parcel. It is finished in four coats of best black enamel on top of rubber solution to prevent rust.

Wheels 26×3 in. flat base, light car type, with spoke holes punched and sunk into the rim at the correct angle for the spoke. Ten-gauge spokes and hubs that do positively prevent dirt getting into the bearings, and do not require constant adjustment. The standard tyres fitted are 26×3 in. Dunlop Magnum.

Transmission By $\frac{5}{8} \times \frac{3}{8}$ in. double strength Hans Renold chain. The chains are not totally enclosed, as this practice is not considered the best with a machine having the speed range of the Brough Superior. Adequate protection is provided, and the lubrication is arranged for the front chain by means of directing the crankcase release on to it. The average life of a set of chains on the Brough Superior is over 10,000 miles.

Tank A fine example of the metal workers' art. It is all 'shape'. No unsightly square corners enter into its construction. It is of the saddle type, and has a very distinctive bulbous nose, arrangements being made to conceal all control wires. The capacity is—petrol $2\frac{1}{2}$ gallons, oil $\frac{1}{2}$ gallon. The petrol tank has two compartments inter-connected through two filter taps to the carburettor. The lubrication arrangements are very neatly carried out in the following manner. Fitted in the top of the tank is a specially designed component, comprising pump plunger, sight feed glass, and quantity regulator. Attached to the underside of the tank is an extension to the plunger, which is connected through a Bowden wire mechanism to a small foot pedal, thus either hand or foot operation is provided in correct quantities, governed by the speed the machine is being driven (not shown in illustrations). The finish is carried out in a choice combination of black and silver, edged with a fine, pure gold-leaf line.

Mudguards 6 in. wide 'D' section light car mudguards are fitted. They are particularly handsome and effective.

Brakes One on each wheel. A Ferodo block is wedged into a 'V' section brake rim on both back and front wheels (illustration does show the modified front brake). They are particularly efficient in action, and rarely require adjustment. The back brake is actuated by a right-hand heel pedal, the front brake from the handlebar.

Handlebars Semi T.T. shape, and carried below the head-securing lock nut. The result from the appearance and riding standpoint is exceedingly pleasing. Two inverted levers are fitted, actuating front brake and exhaust lifter. The centre of the bar is enamelled, as are also all the fittings round the steering head.

Tool Bag A frame tool bag is fitted behind the saddle tube. This fills an otherwise empty space, and is the ideal position for carrying tools free from vibration. A complete set of tools is supplied.

Saddle A special type of Lycett's pan seat is fitted.

Carrier This is extra strong, and quite capable of carrying a passenger.

Stands Front and rear wheel stands are fitted.

Finish The whole machine is superlatively finished, and it is perfectly true to say that in this respect it excels any machine on the market.

The petrol consumption of the 'Brough Superior', Mark I, is 70 miles per gallon, and the oil consumption is 1,200 miles per gallon.

When considering the price of the 'Brough Superior', remember that the maker never intended to produce his design as cheaply as possible. It is a machine made to cater for a connoisseur rider who will have the best and fastest machine on the road.

Such was the specification of what may be called the first luxury motor-cycle to enter the post-war English market. It was a milestone in specifications, and included the first saddle-tank fitted to a motor-cycle, so often copied by competitors short of ideas.

Reverting now to the famous engine. The main design was part of Messrs J. A. Prestwich's post-war development, and was completed by 30 August 1920. Several modifications specified by George were incorporated in later engines supplied to Haydn Road, and these are embodied in the two views reproduced in Fig. 9, the original bearing the important additional title 'Special for Brough'. Some points worthy of note are the centres of the camshafts being set a trifle forward of the cylinder centre line for the front and an equal amount for the back cylinder, four rows of rollers to the big end; heavy ball bearing to the driving end of the crankshaft; and straight rockers very similar to heavy oil-engine practice. The pistons, practically identical with those used today, carried two compression and one scraper rings. Pushrods are short and very light and the valve springs would not shame a Ramsbottom safety valve on a large steam boiler. If any items besides the rockers would date the engine, they are the gudgeon pin end caps and the external valve-lifting mechanism. The remaining features and details I feel are self-evident from the drawing.

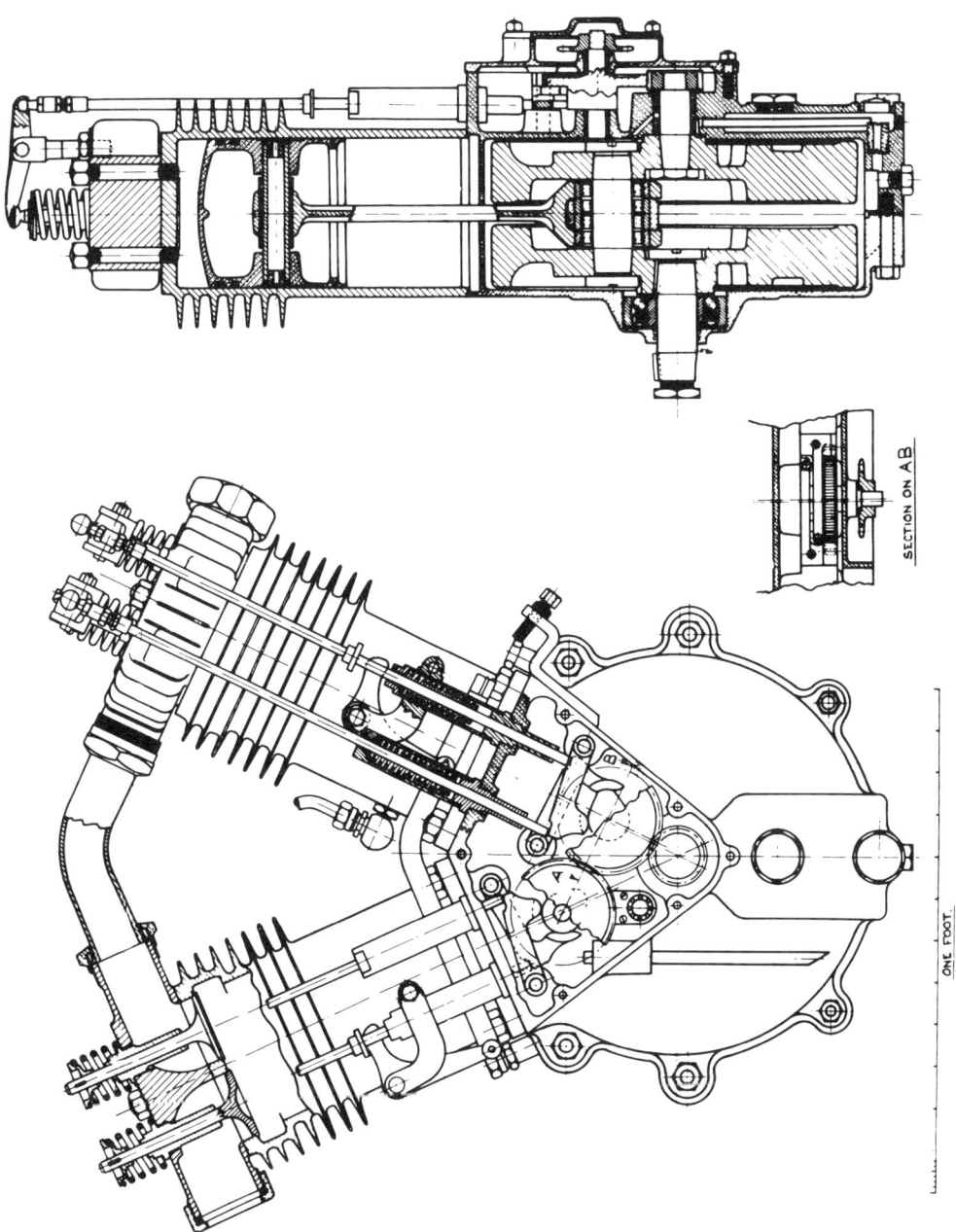

SECTION ON AB

ONE FOOT.

9   *Mechanical details of the '90 Bore' J.A.P. engine*

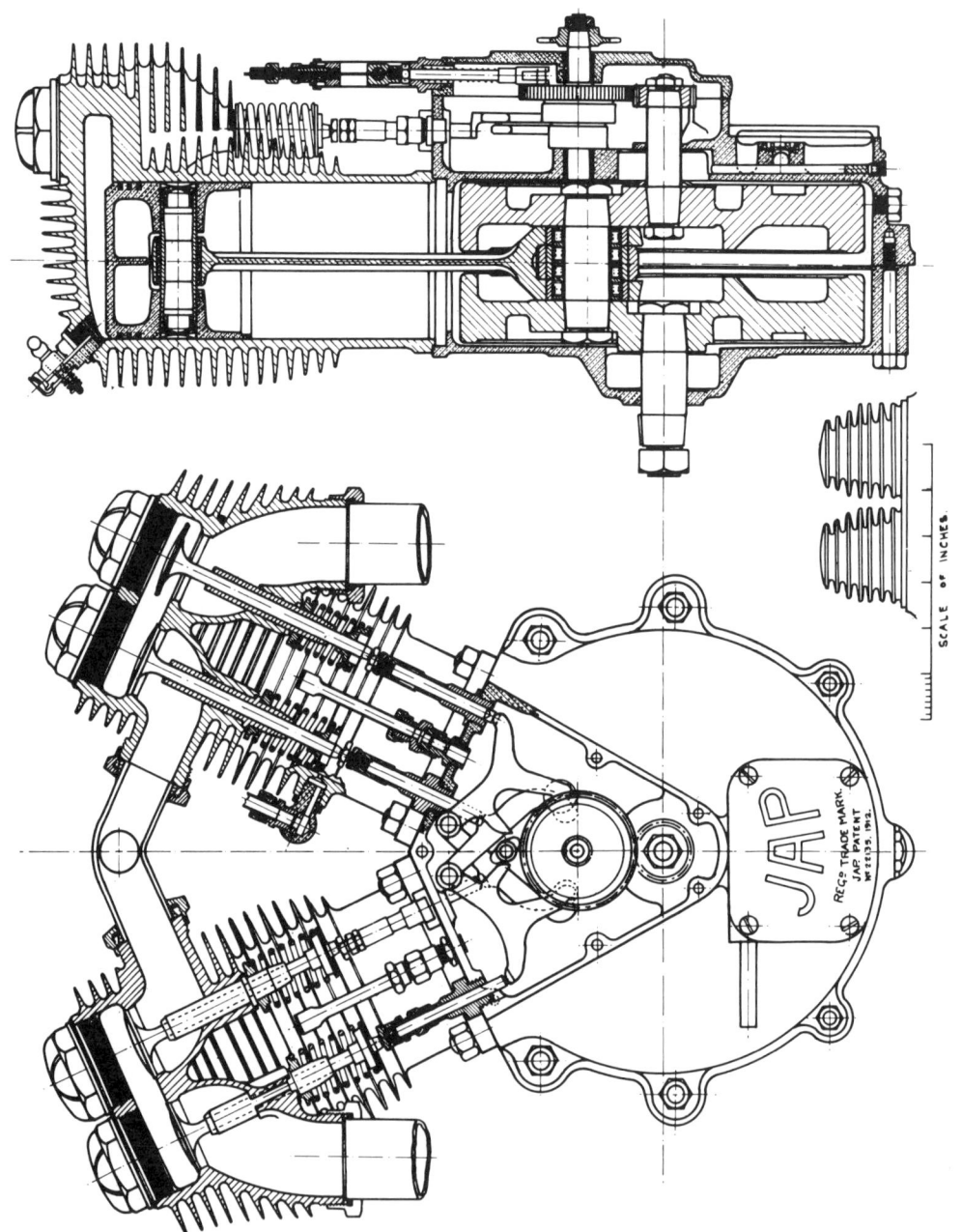

SCALE OF INCHES.

10   *The J.A.P. 1,000 c.c. side-valve engine of 1922*

11   An alternative Brough Superior of 1920 with a M.A.G. engine

Apart from pointing out that the external heat-dissipating ports face right- and left-handed for rear and front cylinders respectively, I think this specification needs no further explanation.

An alternative–side-valve engine was available specially suitable for sidecar work, having cylinders 85·5 × 85 mm. and valves 1¾″ or 2″ diameter, and two views of this milestone of J.A.P. design are included in the drawing shown in Fig. 10, the original being dated 6 January 1922. Unlike the '90 Bore' this unit has only one camshaft bearing the two cams. Both heads are cast integral with the barrels, and access to the 1¾″-diameter valves is through the flat valve caps. As in the '90 Bore' the big end incorporates a four-row roller bearing, with the remainder of the lower works very similar. The detail in Fig. 10 depicts an alternative arrangement utilising aluminium fircone valve caps—and note the plugs in the side of the heads, the compression taps being retained in the same position. The rest of the specification was similar to the overhead-valve machine. The finish was excellent and inspired a reporter to write in December 1920: 'All detail work is beautifully carried out and there is an absence of clips which gladdens the eye of the critic.'

In Fig. 11 we have the Mark II model powered by a long-stroke engine from Geneva made by the Motosacoche à Genève and having cylinders 72 × 90 mm., i.e. 748 c.c. Again I feel it appropriate to follow on with the detailed specification and here it is:

Engine Specially manufactured for the 'Brough Superior', Mark II, by the M.A.G. Engine Co. Bore 72 mm. stroke 90 mm., overhead inlet valves, totally enclosed. Inlet and exhaust valves and exhaust pipes are of large diameter. The cylinder bottoms and all the machined parts of the engine are heavily plated. The exhaust pipes are carried in a very easy sweep to a cast aluminium silencer, thence through a straight extension pipe to the rear. The magneto is chain driven, and is carried at the rear of the back cylinder. Inlet pipe is an aluminium casting. The running of the engine is beautifully quiet and sweet in action. There are no valve gear noises, and the exhaust note is a particularly pleasant hum.

Three-Speed Gear As Mark I.

Carburettor An A.M.A.C. pilot-jet type is found to be the most satisfactory, and this has been standardised.

Ignition As Mark I.

Frame As Mark I.

Wheels As Mark I, except tyres which are Dunlop Heavy, 650 × 65 mm.

Transmission As Mark I.

Tank As Mark I, except that hand pump lubrication only is provided.

Mudguards As Mark I.

Brakes As Mark I.

Handlebars, Tool Bag, Saddle, Carrier, Stands and Finish As Mark I. The petrol consumption on 'Brough Superior', Mark II is 80 miles per gallon. The oil consumption is 1,200 miles per gallon.

Note particularly the forward-facing exhaust ports and pipes, hailed as something new and original just after the Second World War, and the tyre pump nicely tucked away from the vision of thieves along the top tube beneath the tank. In both machines note that we see too an entirely fresh innovation on a motor-cycle—the bulbous-nose saddle tank encompassing the frame top tube as in some locomotives it saddles the boiler, giving a smooth finish and contour to that part of the cycle between the seat and the bars.

A few remarks about these Swiss engines here are most apposite. Known as their type 2C14 they were most beautifully made, the

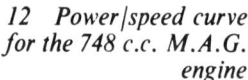

12 Power/speed curve for the 748 c.c. M.A.G. engine

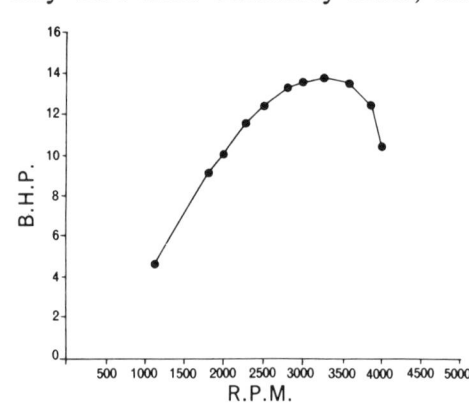

13   Offside prospect of the Brough Superior with the Barr & Stroud engine

barrels were nickel-plated and all other non-ferrous items buffed and polished. In Fig. 12 is reproduced the b.h.p./speed curve for one of these engines, from which one can deduce that the peak brake horse-power was 13·65 at 3,280 r.p.m. Peak revolutions however were 4,000 but with the corresponding output diminished to 10·4 b.h.p. Therefore little would be gained by over-speeding unless on long stretches of down gradients. Each overhead inlet valve had its own cam, and between the two inlet cams was the exhaust or third cam serving both side exhaust valves. Of interest maybe to the vintage owners of these models are the valve settings, which are (1), inlet opens 6 mm. before t.d.c. and closes 12 mm. after b.d.c.; (2), exhaust opens 26 mm. before b.d.c. and closes $\frac{1}{2}$ mm. after t.d.c. Tappet clearances are nil for the inlet and 0·2 mm. for the exhaust valves.

A larger M.A.G. engine could be fitted if specified known as their type 2C9 having a bore and stroke of 82×94 mm., 996 c.c. It is prob-able that a 2C9 engine was fitted in the prototype.

During this period and in 1922–3 a little-known Brough Superior was produced powered by that silent and sweet-running engine the vee-twin sleeve-valve Barr & Stroud, in this instance having cylinders 86×86 mm., 1,000 c.c. and arranged at 50° and known as their WA9. An offside prospect of the bicycle is illustrated

17

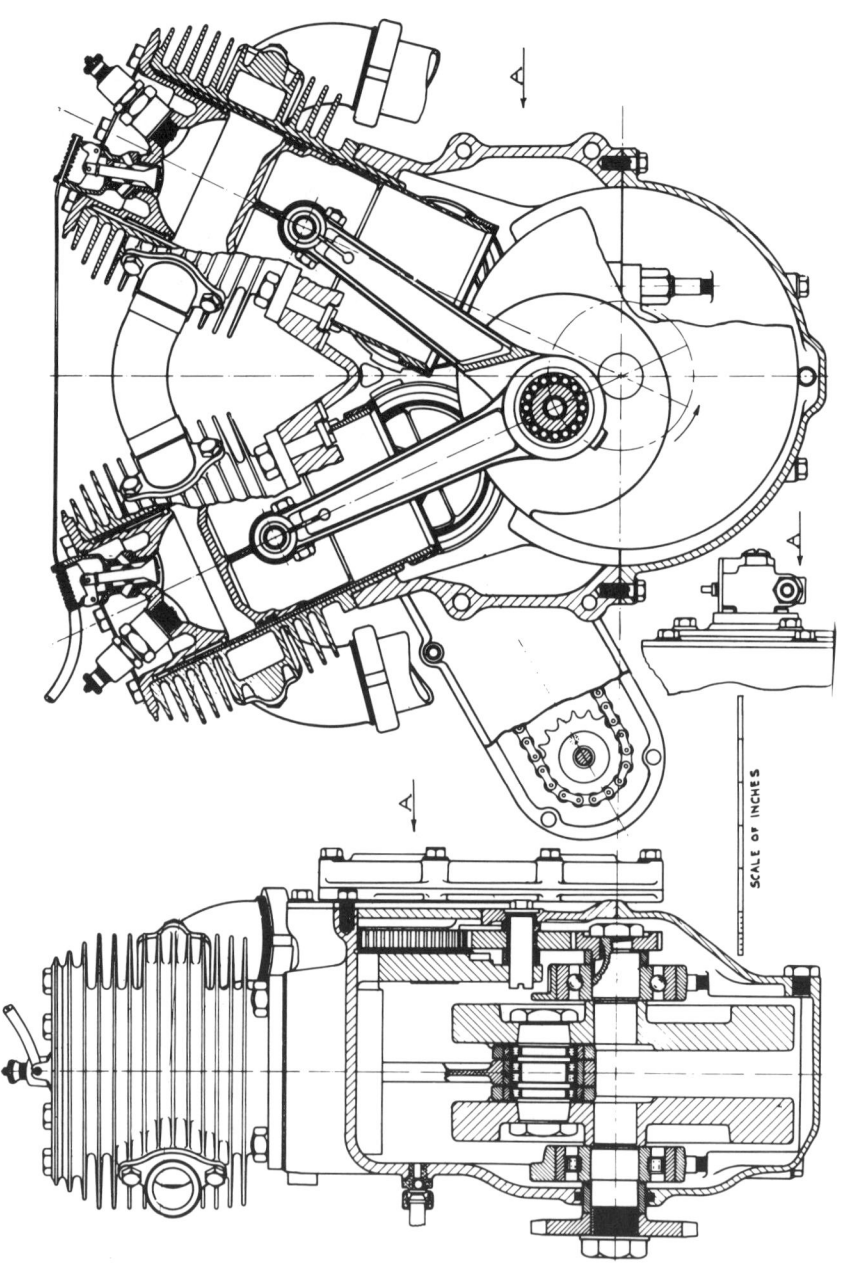

14   General arrangement drawing of the Barr & Stroud vee twin engine

15 Detail of the Barr
& Stroud sleeve valve
operation

in Fig. 13, from which the outline of the engine is clearly shown. At first glance it certainly looks unusual and naturally one wonders what it was like inside, and this is shown in the drawing attached in Fig. 14 giving two sectional views, the elevation being from the near-side so as to be complementary to that in the photograph. Each big end ran on two rows of rollers, the rear rod being the blade rod, and a heavy-duty single-row bearing having rollers $\frac{3}{8}''$ diameter $\times \frac{3}{8}''$ long was employed at the driving, and an equally robust ball bearing at the timing side of the crankshaft. One most unconventional detail is the crankcase, which is split horizontally thus permitting, as the engine builders put it, 'Flywheels, Connecting Rods & Pistons may be removed from the engine without the latter being taken out of the cycle frame'. So let us just ponder over the enormous saving of temper, time and trouble when tackling an engine with a horizontally jointed crankcase. It is always a source of amazement to me that, in spite of the development of the vee twin in respect to its reliability and power output which we shall study on later pages, 'getting at' its internals always demands the engine being removed from the frame, in its turn requiring the dismantling of sundry other items. In this particular I venture to say no improvement took place in forty years in the vee twin at all!

Let us now consider the famous sleeve-valve arrangement made under Messrs Burt & McCullum's patents, listed in Appendix A, and which may be seen in Fig. 15, showing as it does the sleeve together

19

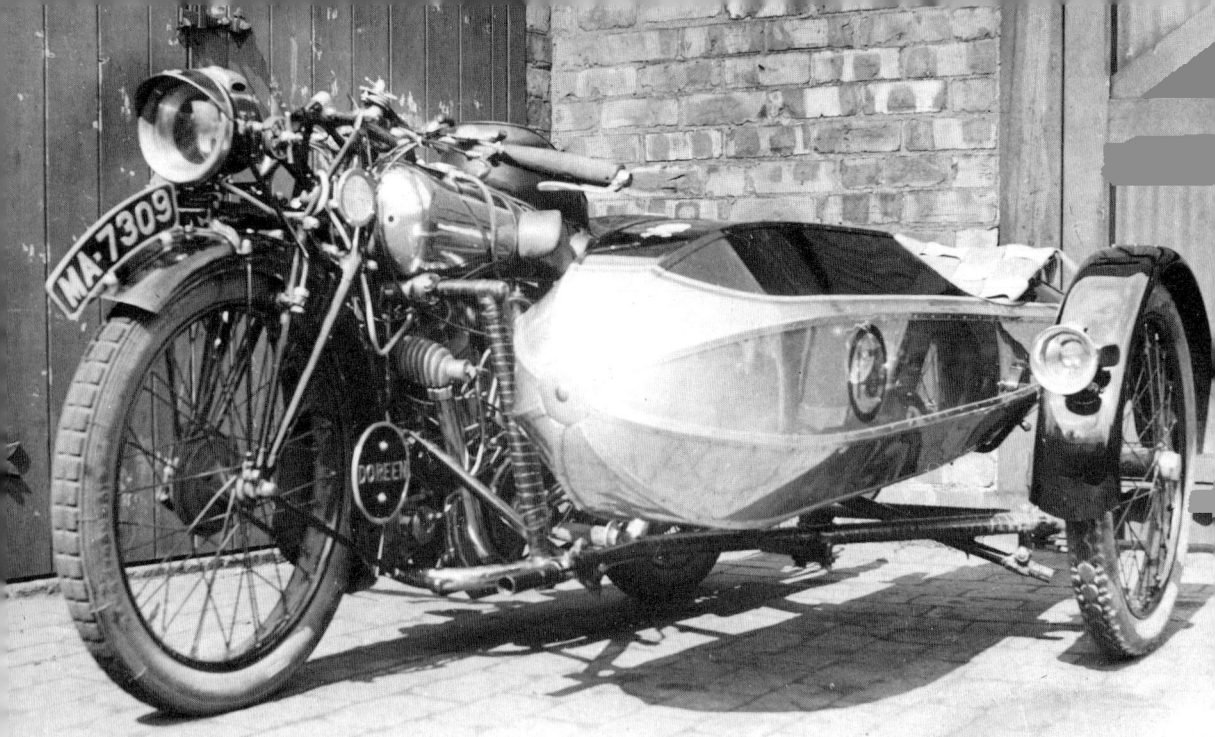

16 *The second Brough Superior built and its 'Torpedo' sidecar*

with its operating mechanism separately and also assembled in a single-cylinder engine suitably sectioned. Made of close-grained cast iron, the sleeve is ground-finished $\frac{8}{64}$″ thick, its lower end terminating in a thickened base carrying a pin at right angles to its axis. Cut in the upper end are five ports specially shaped as a result of experiments. Their position in the sleeve is such that two cover the inlet ports in the cylinder and two the exhaust when at the same time the fifth and larger port opens an inlet and an exhaust port alternately. The pin at the base is actuated by a ball joint placed in the half-speed timing wheel. If now the timing wheel is rotated the sleeve will be not only reciprocated but twisted at the same time so that any point on it will describe an ellipse.

Turning now to the cylinder, this has six ports cut in it which again have been determined experimentally, there being three inlet ports at the top and three exhaust ports opposite. It must be understood that the piston therefore plays no part in the port events, these are taken care of by the sleeve moving outside the piston and within the bore. The half-speed timing wheels are so meshed with the crankshaft pinion that the sleeve and inlet ports begin to coincide just before top dead centre for admission and gradually cease to overlap forming closure of the induction. No ports coincide of course during the compression and firing strokes until the exhaust ports in the sleeve begin to coincide with those in the cylinder at the desired point in the stroke just before bottom dead centre. Naturally ignition is timed normally. Lubrication is by a Best & Lloyd mechanical pump driven off the rear half-speed sleeve shaft.

The great charm and delight in these engines was the total absence of poppet valves, springs, tappets, guides, camshafts and all the noise associated with these impedimenta in motion. Again, less power was absorbed in the sleeves than in the corresponding four valves with stiff springs to be compressed. With such large openings for inlet and exhaust there was less wire-drawing of the induction, better turbulence and more efficient scavenging of the exhaust. It caused *Ixion* in *The Motor Cycle* to write: 'Well silenced and freed from the clack of the usual valve gear, it slides along very amiably.' If it had a defect it was not in the design of the engine but in the lubrication of the sleeve, although I am convinced that with present-day oils and lubrication systems this could be eliminated; and by virtue of its inherent silence, the antagonism of some of the public towards motor-cycles proportionately reduced.

Reverting to Fig. 13 it will be noticed that the remainder of the machine follows familiar Haydn Road practice at this period, including a Sturmey-Archer heavyweight box and Montgomery forks. Use of a sleeve-valve engine again when a more reliable example has become available was not unexpected, bearing in mind the previous attempt seen in Fig. 4, and the two types form an interesting comparison in the development of the sleeve-valve arrangement.

Sidecars had been improved immeasurably since the wicker example we have seen in Chapter I and Fig. 16 illustrates not only a typical 'Torpedo' type of this period but the second Brough Superior built late in 1919 and again fitted with Montgomery forks.

How did these machines perform? Suffice it to record that George Brough won a 'Gold' in the Land's End Trials in 1920, repeated in 1921 and 1922. Additionally he began to receive letters of praise from customers well pleased.

Long ago, on 21 September 1915, *Motor Cycling* described William Brough's creation, the 497 c.c., 65 m.p.h. twin as 'A two-wheeled Rolls Royce'. The past repeats itself and in 1921 George published in his leaflet describing the Mark I and Mark II machines a letter from Mr John Hamilton of Exeter wherein the satisfied customer said 'I certainly think your machine is the Rolls Royce of motor-cycles, and wish you every success in the coming season'.

The successes up to 1922 inspired *The Motor Cycle* when reporting on the make at Olympia in the 30 November issue that year to state for all time 'One would have thought it impossible to add any further refinements to the "SS80" Brough Superior. Yet this Rolls Royce of motor-cycles—it earns the title by something more than mere cost—has been further improved since it made its first (and very successful) appearance in the Six Days Trials.'

From then onwards there followed the obvious and now familiar systasis of terms, so that the Brough Superior was for evermore referred to, with permission from Derby, as *The Rolls Royce of Motor-Cycles*.

CHAPTER III

Enter the SS80 and SS100

A live and progressive entity cannot, because of its very character, remain static and so we find for 1922–3 (1), a new machine entirely the SS80 and (2), the Mark I being the SS80 somewhat simplified as in Fig. 17 and (3), the old Mark II as in Fig. 11.

An offside view of the new SS80 is included in Fig. 22, powered again by a J.A.P. engine with cylinders 85.5×85 mm. or 981 c.c., and a new design of timing gear utilising two camwheels in place of the single cam used previously. Two springs were fitted to each valve, each exhaust pipe was $1\frac{3}{4}''$ bore, the complete specification being recorded in Appendix B.

In the case of the Mark I the engine again is of J.A.P. manufacture and highly-polished inside. The rear brake in this instance was a Ferodo block in the vee-groove rim, the front remaining the internal-expanding type. As the maker said: 'It is a *real* front brake, not merely a fitting to satisfy the law!'

Generally as we have seen the 981 c.c. side-valve engine was fitted in this model but the '90 Bore' o.h.v. engine could be fitted purely for high-speed work.

17   *The first SS80 'MK I S.V.'*

18 Spit and Polish

The Mark II remained very much the same as noticed in Fig. 11 although occasionally cantilever or Montgomery forks were fitted.

As the reader is now aware, the Brough Superior is essentially a luxury machine designed for solo use. As the maker once wrote: 'I knew the public did not want a machine which was virtually a sidecar model, adapted for solo use merely by the fitting of a higher gear. I knew they wanted a type of machine designed from the experienced solo rider's point of view.' The maker's successes at this period amplify most effortlessly what very fine solo cycles they were. On his original racing SS80 colloquially dubbed *Spit and Polish* seen in Fig. 18, the maker made his first appearance at Brooklands in 1922 winning the 5-lap Experts' scratch race, and it was the first side-valve machine to lap this track at 100 m.p.h.

Lessons learnt on this and further outings suggested modifications after which he gained 51 Firsts in a row out of 52 entries, and Fig. 19 depicts the designer-manufacturer-racer astride it in the paddock in its final form, and now affectionately re-christened *Old Bill*. The 52nd race in 1923 ended with *Old Bill* finishing without its rider. As the maker told me, he had experienced slight mis-firing at the Clipstone Meeting near Mansfield during practice and duly shed his gloves and leathers to attend to the trouble. This completed and before he had time to refit his protective clothing he was told to line up for his next race, a standing half-mile. After an excellent start his front tyre burst only forty yards or so short of the finishing line and caused George to slide to the ground with *Old Bill* crossing the line on its own in 20 seconds dead (90 m.p.h.). Most damage however was sustained by the rider who spent many weeks in Mansfield Hospital suffering from severe abrasions to certain tender parts. A little skin grafting was vitally necessary and it was provided by three lads of the Mansfield Motor Cycle Club, strangers to George, who thus proved themselves great sportsmen.

Further light is shed on the risks incidental to high-speed racing by the maker's contribution to the *Nottingham Evening News* in 1937 which I include in full:

RACE TRACK CRASHES AT OVER 100 M.P.H.
By GEORGE BROUGH

The finest riders in the country were assembled in the paddock at Brooklands on the day of the motor-cycle championship in 1923.

In spite of the ear-splitting roar of high-powered and perfectly tuned engines, the anxiety of the last scrutiny before the race began and all the other pre-occupations which crowd into the few tense moments before a big race, I was conscious that my first entry for the championship, 'Old Bill', was attracting a good deal of critical attention.

19 Old Bill

The old stagers were a little contemptuous of his shining finish and scrupulous cleanliness, and they called him 'Spit and Polish'.

Came the line up and the dip of the flag. 'Old Bill' shot away from the mark and flew on his way with gathering speed until a quarter of a mile ahead of his nearest competitor the miles were dissolving into past tense at the rate of nearly two a minute.

On the second lap, an average of 100 m.p.h. was recorded—lap record: 'Old Bill' was walking it!

There were three laps to go—it looked easy. Coming off the Members Bank the third time round, the world stopped turning, and 'Old Bill' and I took over. We shot through the air like a twin comet. . . .

I shall never forget the experience of spinning through the air in a mix-up with the bike and then sliding on the track at over 100 m.p.h. I must have gone a quarter of a circuit after the tyre burst. I was conscious the whole time. As soon as I stopped, I thought of the other fellows coming up behind.

I curled myself up, closed my eyes, covered my head with my arms and crouched there in the middle of the track like an ostrich with its head tucked away in the sand. Then—Whorr-whorr: whorr-whorr-whorr.

It was a miracle they missed. I waited two or three seconds after they had gone. It was a terrible moment, I can tell you. When I thought they were all clear, I jumped up and ran. Old Joe, who still sweeps the track there, suddenly loomed up and I stopped against him.

He looked aghast and said incredulously: 'Crikey! You still alive, sir?'

Then a couple of stewards came round on a combination. One of them said they saw it from the stand and were certain I was mincemeat. He told me to put a coat on and I said I didn't want it. When I looked where he was pointing, I changed my mind and took the coat. The leather was worn clean through and my hand came away covered with blood.

So much for life No. 1.

At Clipstone the same year, I provided more proof that the manu-facturers of tyres were not keeping pace with the manufacturers of engines.

I was riding in the standing start half mile. Again my speed was about 110 when, about 50 yards from the finish the front tyre whipped clean off the rim.

My forearm was hanging by a strip. Thanks to the skill of a surgeon at Mansfield Hospital, I can still use all the muscles in my arm and hand.

I was going down the decline towards the finish when the tyre came off. I was doing 110 at the time and I guess all the crowd saw of me was a cloud of dust and stones.

I remember shooting into the ditch on one side of the track, bouncing out of that, sliding across the track into the other ditch, bouncing out of that and sliding the rest of the way down the centre of the track.

The bike was like a bucking bronco. It went on for 200 yards after crossing the line, ploughing up the surface and creating a dust storm. The muscles and tendons of my forearm were ripped right away.

My time for the standing start for that trip was exactly 18 [*sic*] seconds.

The amusing (!) part about it was that Freddie Dixon who is now one of my greatest friends, but used to be my greatest rival, was a bit upset when somebody suggested that the prize should go to me.

An official told him that although he had clocked the fastest time *officially*, actually my machine had crossed the line in 2½ seconds less.

'Yes, but the man wasn't on it,' said Freddie. 'You might as well run these races by firing the bikes out of a gun!'

The injuries to the rider are rather graphically described. After such treatment the forearm would be limp and flaccid and give the feeling to the patient at the time that it was indeed just hanging. The tendons would be joined by the surgeon permitting later use of the limb. Nevertheless it is a particularly enlightening description of high-speed work in the early 1920's and possibly new to many readers.

A few details of this historic machine *Old Bill* may not be out of place. Having a bore and stroke of 85×85 mm. the total swept volume was 981 c.c., the angle between the cylinders being $50°$. The timing gear utilised four cams, its rating was 8 h.p. and Stanley Greening informed me it actually produced a little more than 40 b.h.p. Modifications included machining away the top of the crankcase so that the cylinder-base flanches are slightly below the top level of the timing chest, thus giving a compression ratio a little higher than normal, and deep valve-cavity caps. Both connecting rods were undrilled but lightened and all the internals were highly polished. Each flywheel was machined from the steel billet, connection between the rim and the centre being by one diametrical spoke, this spoke housing at its centre the mainshaft, and nearer the circumference, the crankpin. Incidentally the usual disc flywheels were fitted to standard engines. The gearbox was a heavyweight Sturmey-Archer, the forks being racing Webb, and note the additional side strutting of the frame. Main and big-end bearings were all roller, the cam followers being solid.

Eventually this historic bicycle was sold and used by two or three different owners, one running it disgraced by an enormous sidecar. During the last war it was bombed in a Kensington mews and now has been acquired and restored by C. E. Allen, Esq., of the Brough Superior Club.

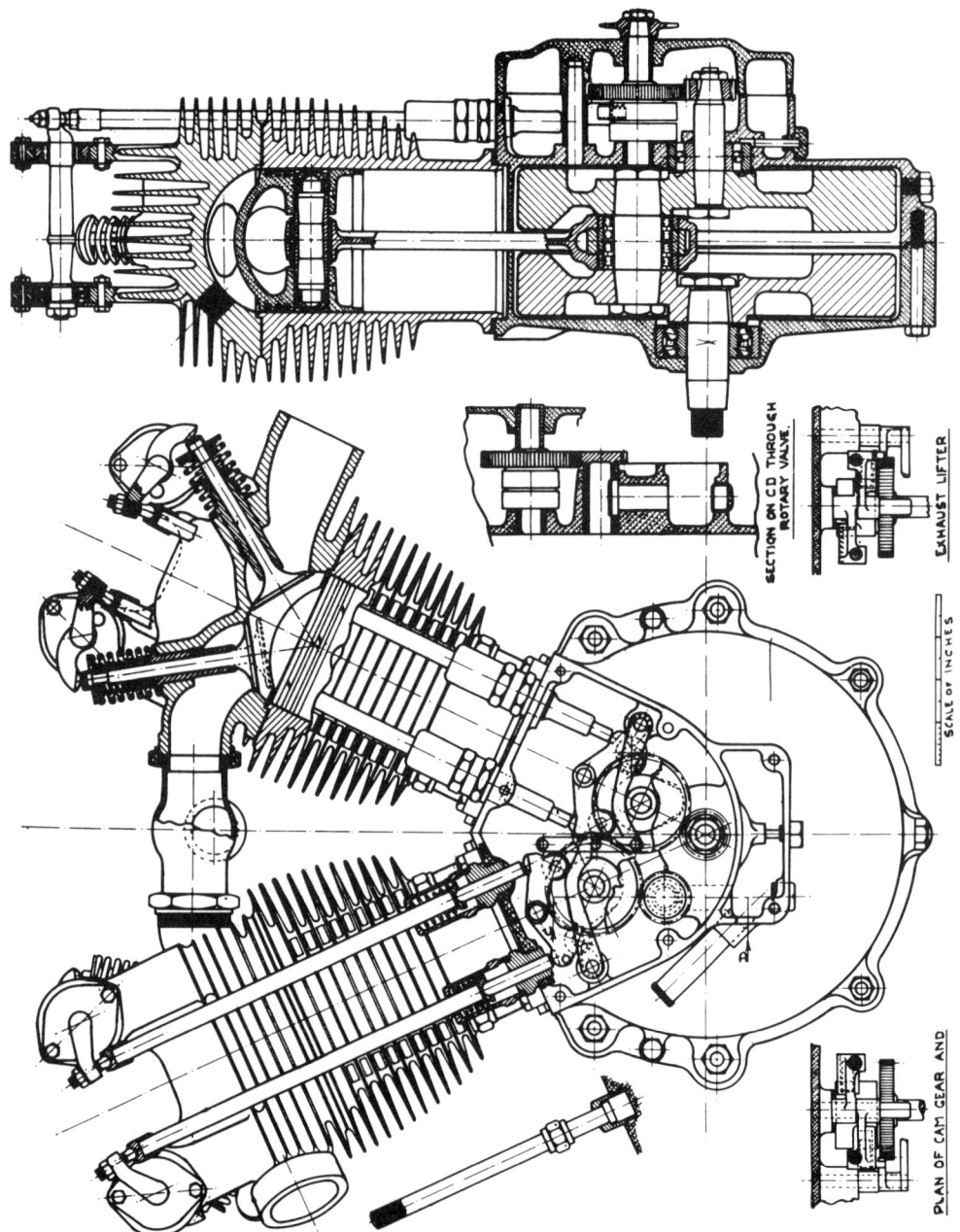

SECTION ON C D THROUGH
ROTARY VALVE.

EXHAUST LIFTER

SCALE OF INCHES

PLAN OF CAM GEAR AND

20   The o.h.v. 980 c.c. J.A.P. engine of 1924

21 One of the first SS100's

During 1923–4 it was resolved to redesign the o.h.v. machine, incorporating latest developments of the Tottenham factory in the matter of big twins, exemplified by the new engine of 85·7 × 85 mm. cylinders equivalent to 980 c.c. Development work on this using the old '90 Bore' as a basis had occupied practically two years, and from the drawings reproduced in Fig. 20 dated 1924 it will be seen there are four cams mounted on two camshafts, the last named now arranged on the centre lines of the cylinders, not slightly offset as we have seen in the '90 Bore'. A change of equal importance is to be found in the design of the overhead gear. Gone are the heavy oil-engine-type lever rockers, and supplanting them are long transverse rockers mounted in a single-row ball bearing each and spaced at $3\frac{3}{8}''$ centres, these being housed in lugs cast integral with the cylinder heads. The heads proper are made hemispherical internally and contain two valves at 45° to each other, the pistons now being much shorter, with domed heads and three compression rings. Two springs are fitted to each valve and lubrication was by a mechanical oil pump, and 1,450 m.p.g. was claimed by the works, a figure confirmed by my own experience with an engine of this period. Some engines a little later in 1924 and onwards had the rockers mounted in needle roller bearings.

22　*The 1922/3 SS80*

To house this hefty power unit a frame of bottom loop or cradle construction was conceived in collaboration with the late Herbert le Vack, one essential feature being the complete exclusion of any loose clip or clips, and the complete machine is shown in Fig. 21.

Three speeds, the generated gears being of 120-ton steel, were incorporated in the Sturmey-Archer special heavyweight box with hand change, the pivot being mounted on the box itself. What memories the long lever with black ebony knob engenders, memories of hand use for first and second gears and, as the knob lowered, using one's toe for selecting top! And of course that handy toe again for sliding quickly into second. In this guise there was exhibited for the first time in 1924 at Olympia what the maker was pleased to call the SS100. Now a little quotation from the 1925 catalogue, one of many cherished records in the writer's collection: 'Every SS100 will be despatched with a written guarantee, signed by the Maker, that the Machine has actually been timed over 100 m.p.h. for a quarter of a mile. A Private Road, 1¾ miles long has been very kindly offered to the Manufacturer for the purpose of this guarantee.'

Seen in Fig. 22 is the contemporary SS80, utilising now the same frame as its faster brother and girder forks; a Timken roller bearing was fitted to the steering to obviate indentation as when balls were used. Note the alternative system or layout of exhausting where two alloy ribbed ports were fitted to the cylinders and leading to separate pipes brought well to the rear of the machine, each carrying an aluminium silencer, dubbed 'lamp glass' silencers on account of their shape and outline.

THE CASTLE FORK

(Pat. No. 3942)

THE SPEEDMAN'S IDEAL.

Now being marketed in such form as to be adaptable to most standard machines.

The Fork is entirely a British Production throughout, and has been perfected over prolonged and strenuous tests, so that it can be offered as the very last word in steering apparatus.

For further particulars and Order Form
apply to The

CASTLE FORK & ACCESSORIES Co.,
HAYDN ROAD, NOTTINGHAM.

23   Details of the famous Castle forks

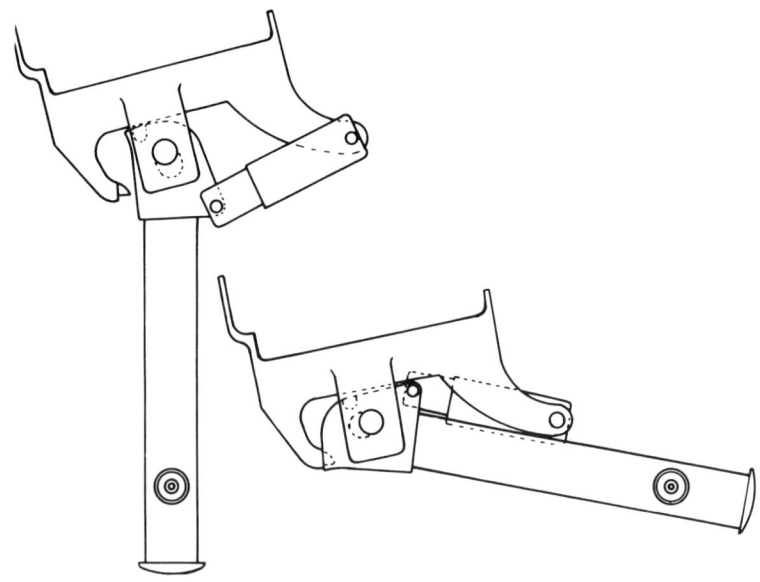

24   Two views of the Karslake-Brough prop stand

As in the case of the SS100, flat-base rims with two security bolts
were used, $26 \times 3''$ for the SS80 and $28 \times 3''$ for the former, the wheel
hubs having adjustable roller bearings. Solo gear ratios were 3·5,
5·2 and 10·1 to 1. Again lubrication was by mechanical pump but
with a handpump also for an extra supply in any emergency, and
Lucas electric lighting was a standard fitting.

Thus the range for 1925 was now:

MK I S.V. MK II S.V. } Not advertised	
SS80 fully equipped	£150
SS80 magneto model only	£140
SS100 magneto model only standard	£170

and of a very high finish indeed.

Reverting to Fig. 21 the reader will notice that a parallel-ruler
design of fork, instead of the girder type on the SS80, is fitted, which
came to be known as the 'Castle' fork. Provisionally protected by
Patent No. 3941 of 24 January 1925 in the joint names of George
Brough and Harold Karslake, it was made in the Haydn Road Works
but sold by the Castle Fork & Accessories Company—the two partners
being the two joint patentees—to the industry as and when required.
As a matter of interest there is reproduced in Fig. 23 the relevant

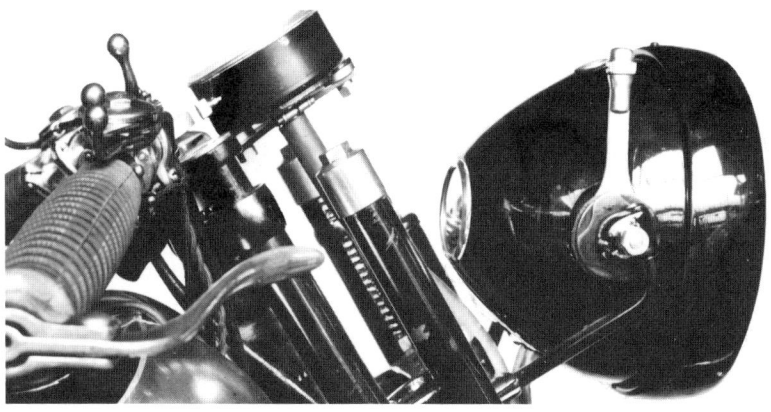

25 *Pictorial view of the dipper*

page from a double leaflet issued by this subsidiary, and it is interesting to compare Figs. 21 and 23. In the latter figure improved side shock-absorbers have replaced the triangular set on the first SS100, and on a later and final design as for example in Fig. 56 the long coil-spring tubes have been shortened. The very term 'Castle forks' suggests to the connoisseur hair-line steering and cornering as if the wheels were flanged and running on rails at any speed; deflection was reasonably limited, and so very positive compared with the spongy over-rated fittings called forks today. Other factors to be reckoned with are that the trail of a Castle fork remains constant and there is practically no alteration in the wheelbase when the fork is working. With ordinary girder types there may be an appreciable variation in the wheelbase adversely affecting cornering at high speed. Again, should one tube of a Castle fork become damaged it is cheaper for a good repair specialist to insert another than it is to replace the complete tubular sliding fork which is now so often necessary. Harold Karslake sized things up by stating 'I am convinced that it would be extremely difficult to find a fitting equal to the Castle fork for high speeds on heavy machines'.

Two other accessories could be obtained by the industry from this minor company, viz. the Castle Prop Stand and the Castle Lamp Dipper Attachment, the former protected by Patent No. 256,373 of 12 August 1926 in the names of the two partners and the latter protected by Patent Application No. 866 of 12 January 1926 in the same names. Fig. 24 illustrates two views of the prop stand listed at 25*s*., and it is pleasing to note that the original made by Harold Karslake is now the Karslake Trophy, B.S. Club. It is a perfect boon, especially on a heavyweight machine, and comes into its own when gates, etc., necessitating two stops have to be opened, as I can testify. In Fig. 25 we have a detailed view of the Dipper, and it was available for the Lucas 462 acetylene and the corresponding electric headlamp. Later, with universal electric lighting and the twin-filament bulb, the device became superseded. Its cost price ready for fitting by the purchaser was a modest 10s. 6d.

I feel this is the appropriate place to lay bare the secrets of the J.A.P. nomenclature, as much as been said so far about these engines.

The symbols and number were stamped on top of the valve-chest cover or on the top of the crankcase adjacent, and comprised two groups usually arranged like a large fraction. The numerator gave brief particulars of the engine followed by a /. After the / the letter denoted the year of manufacture. The denominator would give the number in figures followed also by a / and after the /, the symbol denoting anything special. Considering first the symbols, they are as follow:

O=Overhead valve.
T=Twin cylinders.
R=Racing.
S=Sports—short stroke only.
C=Sports.
W=Water-cooled.
Z=Dry-sump lubrication.
Y=Double exhaust port.
V=175 c.c. s.v. 60×62 mm.
Z=175 c.c. s.v. 55×73 mm.
N=200 c.c. s.v. 55×83 mm.
B=250 c.c. s.v. 64·5×76 mm.
A=300 c.c. s.v. 70×78 mm.
I=350 c.c. s.v. 70×90 mm.
K=500 c.c. s.v. 85·7×85 mm.
L=550 c.c. s.v. 85·7×95 mm.
U=600 c.c. s.v. 85·7×104 mm.
GT=680 c.c. Twin, s.v. 50°. 70×88 mm.
MT=750 c.c. Twin, s.v. 50°. 70×97 mm.
KT=980 c.c. Twin, s.v. 50°. 85·7×85 mm.
KTCY=980 c.c. Twin, s.v. 50°. 8/30. 85·7×85 mm.
LT=1100 c.c. Twin, s.v. 60°. 85·7×95 mm.
DT=1323 c.c. Twin, s.v. 60°. 90×104 mm. Used on rail trolleys and target-towing trolleys. These were 1100 c.c. Twin 60° and air-cooled.

O was always used to denote an o.h.v. engine and we have:
HO=175 c.c. o.h.v. 53×78 mm.

TO = 200 c.c. o.h.v. 57 × 78 mm.
PO = 250 c.c. o.h.v. 62·5 × 80 mm.
YTO = 500 c.c. o.h.v. Twin. 60 × 88 mm.
POR = 250 c.c. Racing (up to 1933). 62·5 × 80 mm.
NOR = 250 c.c. Racing (1950 onwards). 65·5 × 74 mm.
BOR = 250 c.c. T.T. Racing (1934 and 1935). 64·5 × 76 mm.
SOC = 350 c.c. Sports. Short stroke. 74 × 80 mm.
SOR = 350 c.c. Racing. Short stroke. 70 × 80 mm.
IOR = 350 c.c. Racing. Long stroke. 70 × 90 mm.
KOC = 500 c.c. Sports. Shortened stroke. 85·7 × 85 mm.
KOR = 500 c.c. Racing. Shortened stroke. 85·5 × 85 mm.
JOR = 500 c.c. Racing. Long stroke. 80 × 99 mm.
PTOR = 500 c.c. Racing twin. 62·5 × 80 mm.
KTOR = 980 c.c. o.h.v. Racing. 8/45. 85·7 × 85 mm.
JTOR = 998 c.c. o.h.v. Racing. 8/50. 80 × 99 mm.
GTO = 680 c.c. o.h.v. 70 × 88 mm. (674 c.c.)
KTO = 980 c.c. o.h.v. 8/45. 85·7 × 85 mm.
JTO = 8/50 (touring version of JTOR). 80 × 99 mm.

For speedway and sprint engines the following were employed:
SOS = 350 c.c. o.h.v. Grass track. 74 × 80 mm.
JOS = 500 c.c. 80 × 99 mm.
JTOS = 80/8 o.h.v. Twin. Sprint. 80 × 99 mm. A few **8/75**'s were made with dry sump, symbols JTOSZ.
W/W = 1,100 c.c. o.h.v. Mark I Racing engine. Lubrication by gear pump.

So much for what the symbols mean before the first /. After the / the symbol or letter tells us the year of manufacture according to the following code:

P N E U M A T I C S   W H Y Z D R V F O G
1920 1 2 3 4 5 6 7 8 9   1930 1 2 3 4 5 6 7 8 9

Now let us see how far we have got. An engine with the numerator LTZ/O would mean an 1,100 c.c. s.v. dry-sump twin built in 1938. With KTORW/Z the engine would be a 1933 980 c.c. racing twin, water-cooled. The reader can now tell at a glance what type of engine he has and its age.

Considering the denominator, this could be written as a simple number thus: 12345. It could have after it a / and after the / another symbol. These were known as deviation symbols covering a specific modification during a production year. In the world of J.A.P. the production year ran from 1 September to 31 August following. A list of deviation symbols is as follows:

A = High lift cam.
B = Modified gearcover and exhaust lifter for rear drive 300 c.c. and 350 c.c. 'Roadster'.
C = Crankcase with inclined platform, Cologne. L Mke. Two stroke.
D = Cast iron piston, flat top, fitted to standard engine.

35

E=Cast iron piston, dished top, fitted to standard engine.

F=Aluminium piston domed top, fitted to standard engine.

G=Gear spindle, ball bearing when fitted as alternative to phosphor bronze.

H=Pulley spindle, roller bearing when fitted as alternative to phosphor bronze or ball bearing.

J=Roller-type camlevers and exhaust lifter to suit 500 and 600 c.c. s.v.

K=Special chainline requirement for pulley spindle.

L=O/T flywheel and screw-on sprocket, flange type, for two strokes.

M=Crankcase without oilbox.

N=Magneto sprocket for type NA, M.L. magneto. Two strokes.

O=Cylinder No. 2 type.

P=Cylinder No. 4 type.

R=Cylinder No. 3 type, and sometimes rotary oil breather.

S=Double-row roller big-end bearing. 250 and 350 c.c. o.h.v. racing engines.

T=New-type crankcase and rotary valve. 500 and 600 c.c. s.v. singles.

U=Modifications for new tappet centres. 350 c.c. s.v. roadster.

V=Reduced centre connecting rods giving lower-compression engine.

Y=1924 pattern crankcase converted to rotary valve.

*=Refer to engine record card.

These symbols were used over a period from 1921 to 1925.

After this period S or * after the / in the numerator would mean the customer's specification only and would have one or more parts not standard, the * denoting a specially prepared engine for record attempts or rider's requirements and specially tuned.

Now racing had played an integral and important part in the development of the SS100 and in eradication of the inevitable teething troubles and for the record, let us note that prior to this machine appearing at Olympia, Herbert le Vack had attained 123 m.p.h. solo and 103 m.p.h. with sidecar on a French road. In winning the 200 miles solo and sidecar races at Brooklands he created nine world's records. Other successes included the 100 miles Welsh T.T. at Pendine, all three 50 miles races at Southport besides gold awards in the London–Edinburgh, Land's End and similar trials.

A journalist summed it up conclusively by writing: 'The latest SS100 is not only a thing of beauty, but it is also a most charming motor-cycle to ride.'

As an illuminating conclusion to this chapter I would add that the engine in *Old Bill* bears the symbols KTR/E.

CHAPTER IV

The *Alpine Grand Sports*, the *Pendine* and two **Fours**

For serious road work even with a superior performance, lights and normal fittings were really necessary even at this period (1925–6), so it was decided at Haydn Road to produce a sporting version of the SS100 using the increased output of power from an engine developed from the racing successes of Le Vack; in other words, an even better SS100.

This new creation would require a modified frame and shortened wheelbase, electric lighting, small racing windscreen, large pannier bags for the high-speed touring rider and a maximum of over 100 m.p.h. In the design of the cycle as a whole the maker was helped in several details by his friend Harold Karslake who, let me now say, had purchased the fifth Brough Superior made in the Stockhill House Lodge days. Now Karslake had built the original *Dreadnought* in 1903 and in addition to being an authority on lubrication was a mechanical engineer of great ability. On one or two occasions in the distant past, due to a little over-oiling, an amount of lubricant finally settled on Harold's legs giving rise to the soubriquet 'Oily' which he rather treasured.

After a small portion of the works had been set aside, work commenced on creating the new frame for the new engine by the frame builder aided by Karslake. After a few days the complete bicycle, minus plating, paint and lamps, was offered with no little trepidation to George, who had religiously kept out of that corner of the works! Then for four days he and a henchman were missing but eventually turned up—full of praise! It took the form of orders for the prototype bicycle to be enamelled, plated and made otherwise presentable for the Olympia Show in eleven days' time! Fig. 26 depicts this masterpiece—the first-ever *Alpine Grand Sports*.

A detailed study of the published specification discloses that the new J.A.P. engine of 985 c.c. had cylinders 80 × 99 mm., three springs to each valve, and roller bearings throughout which had been the pushrods themselves are not yet enclosed, as will be noticed

26　*First* Alpine Grand Sports *of all time*

in Fig. 26, and the first modified design of Castle forks fitted, this permitting the front wheel to be the only unsprung item. A new development, putting an end for ever to fiddling with wheel adjustments, were heavy-duty ball journal bearings to each wheel, and of course with front knock-out spindles. How after this progressive step any other motor-cycle produced could have had such obsolete items as adjustable wheel bearings is something which has always appalled me. Eight-inch diameter rear and $5\frac{1}{2}''$ front brakes were built into each hub, tyres were $28'' \times 3\frac{1}{2}''$ wired on and rear spokes, to stand the output of such a big engine, were no less than 8 s.w.g., although insulated to an excellent degree by the Enfield-type rear cush sprocket. Previous gear ratios of 3·5, 5·2 and 10·1 to 1 having been found eminently suitable for fast road work were retained in the Sturmey-Archer heavy-weight box, but here the gate change is mounted on the top tube beneath the right-hand bar just handy for the hand to drop on it. Incidentally for racing different and close ratios could be supplied. A few other attractive features were a wheelbase of 58″, a tank capacity of four gallons, bars 32″ wide overall and 6″ mudguards. The frame, wheels, forks and similar items were treated to one coat of weatherproof rubber covering primer followed by four coats of black stove enamel. All plating was deposited on an initial layer of copper with the top of the tank black but edged with a gold-leaf line $\frac{1}{8}''$ wide. Plating on a prepared copper surface is the only effective and lasting method which, with no little advantage, could be emulated in present-day productions.

Here I think we will return to Fig. 26 for a few moments. The far background most will recognise as the office of the old Haydn Road Works. The bicycle is shown before it was cleaned and inspected immediately after the maker had returned from participating in the Alpine Trial, which he finished off by making fastest time in the Katzburg Hill Climb, thus securing the cup for the best performance in the trial. The late F. P. Dickson rode an SS100 in the same event, winning the cup for the best performance by an amateur and another for making fastest time in the Mont Cénis Hill Climb. George brought the cup home but struck trouble with H.M. Customs. Although it had been honourably won and acquired heavy duty was demanded. After months of fruitless argument back and forth with inelastic officialdom, all hope of getting it to Nottingham was abandoned and its present fate is unknown. Such a typical way of treating those who help the country's reputation! Those cups enjoying pride of place on the saddle are Dickson's. Previously the maker had competed in the London–Edinburgh Trial earlier this year (1925).

Forming the immediate background in Fig. 26 are from left to right our friends George Smith, Ike J. Webb, the late Donald Webb and Jack Browning.

In the 1930 International Six Days Trial F. P. Dickson started as No. 11, Eddy Meyer as No. 19 and George Brough as No. 43. Both Dickson and Brough unfortunately had accidents, both breaking legs. Brough was in collision with a large American car driven by a woman and completely on its wrong side, the impact being great enough to throw him over the car. He instituted proceedings for damages, when it transpired the defendant had been driving only a few days! George was awarded 150,000 francs damages in 1933. Sad to relate F. P. Dickson sustained a crushed ankle during this trial. Failure to have it amputated led to pneumonia setting in which proved fatal. George attended the funeral of his old friend. Dickson, connected with the Wilkinson Sword Company, was a resident of Melrose and his mount was an SS100 with sprung frame new on 16 April 1930.

A derivative of the *Alpine Grand Sports* was the *Pendine*, named after the successes achieved by the tuned SS100 at Pendine. It

27 A Pendine *with Eddy Meyer in the saddle*

housed this tuned J.A.P. engine using a higher compression ratio, had narrower bars and a magneto only. It had in addition a guarantee that it had exceeded 110 m.p.h. In Fig. 27 we have a fine example of the *Pendine* machine with Eddy Meyer in the saddle. This famous rider by 1928 had won over eighty Firsts in Austria and this celebrated bicycle was fitted with the JTOR J.A.P. engine. Note too the bulbous-nosed saddle tank now reinforced by three strengthening bands enhancing its general effect of robustness, but without detracting from the fundamental smoothness of line.

Here it is nice to record that the combination of the bracing Pendine air and the stimulating successes of the *Pendine* machine provided so many happy occasions for the maker that in sheer felicity, exuberance and suggestions from Mrs Brough, he later gave his house in Redhill, Nottinghamshire the name PENDINE! Thus is the deep humanity of a man revealed.

List prices of the *Alpine Grand Sports* and *Pendine* were £170 and £165 respectively. Thus in the *Alpine Grand Sports* we have what was previously a 'bare' SS100 now invested in full road-going equipment and with no extras. For racing of course the affluent used the *Pendine*. Many of us, younger men at this period, were not affluent and therefore merely gazed rapt in adoration of the catalogue illustrations with which we had to be content!

Had one saved in a methodical way then by 1927 there was available the Overhead 680, 'The Miniature SS100' as George described it and which first encountered the public gaze at Olympia in 1926, and was in full production first in 1927. It is to be seen in Fig. 28. For many years Tottenham had produced a side-valve engine of 70×88 mm., 674·4 c.c. to be really accurate, from which the o.h.v. version was of course developed. Compared with the *Alpine Grand Sports*, its wheelbase was reduced to 56″ and it would do 80 m.p.h. solo, the capacity of the naturally smaller tank equalling 2½ gallons with half a gallon of oil in a separate compartment. A mechanical oil pump and bevel driven magdyno as on the A.G.S. completed the specification. With a magdyno it was listed at 103 guineas but with magneto only at 96 guineas.

Further details, which will provide some extra pleasure I hope, of this new engine, will be found in the drawings dated 11 June 1926 shown in Fig. 29. It is a standard 2-cam engine with open pushrods and unenclosed rockers and, as I hinted in a previous sentence, was a smaller version of the SS100 engine. Later, in all the o.h.v. twins the pushrods and rockers became enclosed as shown in the detail in Fig. 29, which represents the enclosure used on the 500 c.c. o.h.v. twin engine, the original being dated 13 September 1930.

28   *The first type of Overhead 680*

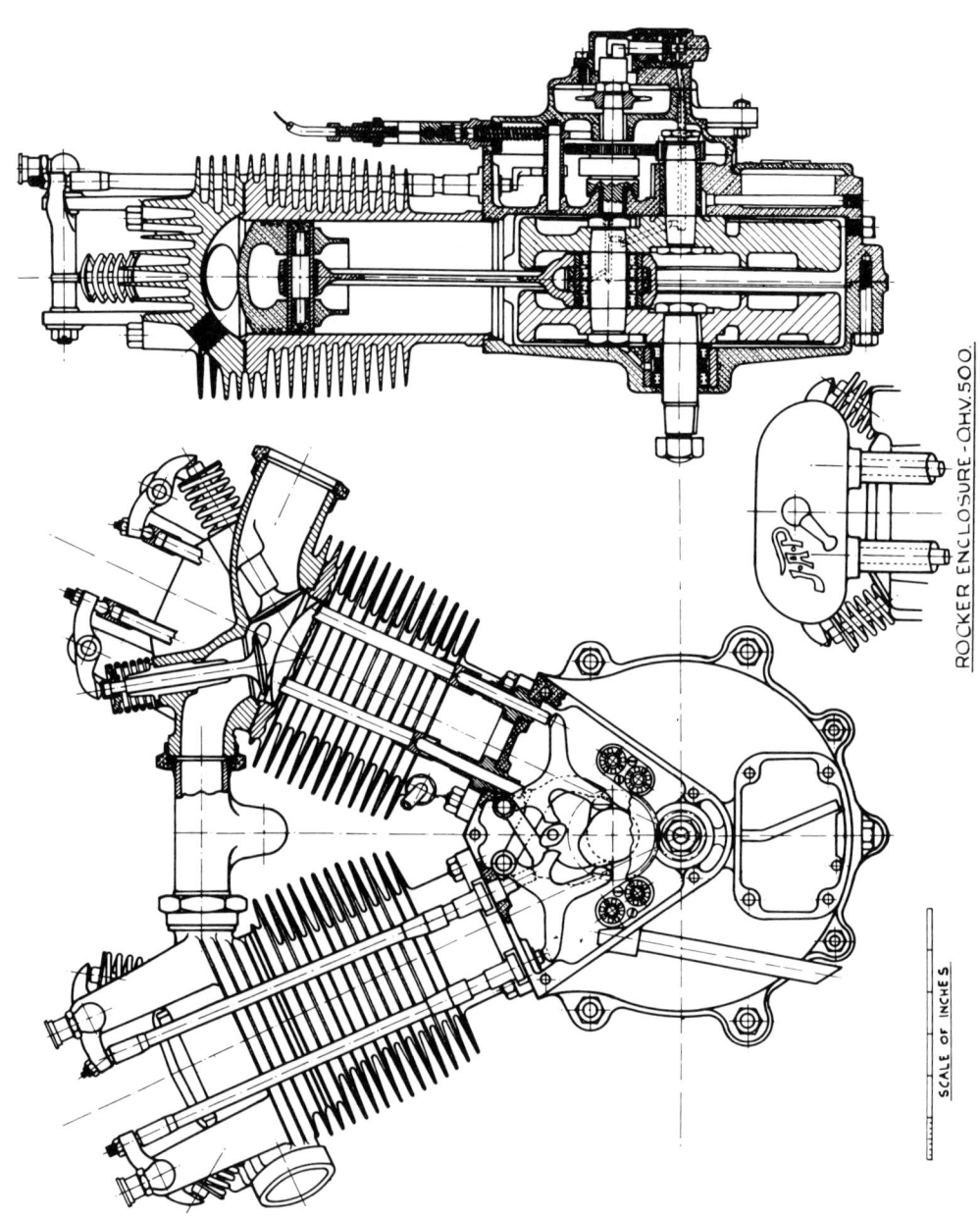

ROCKER ENCLOSURE - O.H.V. 500

SCALE OF INCHES

29   *Drawings of the 1926 o.h.v. 680 c.c. J.A.P. engine*

42

30　*View of the new 750 c.c. Side Valve*

First such enclosure on the 1,000 c.c. was dated 27 October 1928 and on the o.h.v. 680 in November 1928. There has been some previous speculation as to when such refinements appeared and I trust these dates will solve the mystery.

Basically for 1927 the well-tried SS80 remained very much the same as in Fig. 22 but with Castle forks in place of the original girders. Really two examples were available, the 'Standard' having the 2-cam engine developing 25 b.h.p. and the '*de Luxe*' with the 4-cam developing 30 b.h.p. It had been the maker's assumption all along that a big engine normally working at only a fraction of its maximum output will give better service than a smaller one nearly always pressed to near its limit. Such an assumption was proved on many occasions, as for example by the owner, who wrote, unsolicited, to say that in 63,427 miles he had not had one involuntary stop, and spares had cost a mere £1 7s. 1d.! With the 4-cam engine its list price was £130, in standard form £122 10s., also if in standard form but with magneto and bulb horn only the cost was £115.

How popular was the silent and docile side-valve engine in these days may be gleaned from a study of Figs. 30 and 31 depicting the 750 side valve first shown in 1927 and having cylinders 70 × 97 mm. or 746 c.c., and with roller bearings throughout. In describing it as 'The SS80's Younger Brother' the manufacturer went on to say 'The Engine is extraordinarily quiet, whilst the silencing arrangements give a *soft low note* so pleasing to the ear. It will do 70–75 m.p.h. and the very minimum of attention is necessary to keep it in tune. A charming machine for the fast long-distance tourist.' Other features calculated to endear it to the enthusiast were a fuel consump-

31 Another view of the new 750 c.c. machine

tion of 80 m.p.g., and the oil used was a gallon for 1,500 miles. Note the bevel-driven magdyno and large box-type alloy silencer very much connected with that *soft low note*! The remainder of the bicycle-frame, wheels, forks and gearbox, etc., were as used on the Overhead 680. Its price was 97 guineas fully equipped but the magneto-only model could be had for 90 guineas.

This year, 1927, was a memorable Brough year for another reason —the introduction of yet another side valve, this being a vee four of which two side views appear in Figs. 32 and 33. Having a bore and stroke of 58×91 mm., 994 c.c., the angle between the cylinders was 60° with a single camshaft between them. Each cylinder was cast separately and, like the 1934 SS100, deeply spigoted into the crank-

32 Side view of the impressive Vee Four

44

33 *Another prospect of the Vee Four*

case for rigidity. H-section connecting rods were preferred, the big
ends being split. The front end of the camshaft drove the distributor,
ignition being by accumulator and coil. Transmission was from the
engine through a single-plate clutch in a large flywheel, the gearbox
being of normal design and containing four ratios of 4, 5, 6 and 10
to 1, and this and further interesting details will be seen from a study
of the diagrams shown in Fig. 34. To reduce slightly the overall
length of the transmission the final bevel drive had the bevel wheel
facing forward, thus bringing the sprocket spindle a little further
towards the engine. Both generator and speedometer were driven
from the gearbox, tyres were 26″ × 3·25″, both brakes were 8″ diameter
and the whole machine was a trifle smaller than the contemporary
SS100.

Originally it had been the maker's intention to produce an engine
based on the Lancia patents, but this the car manufacturers would not
allow. Had they done so the included angle between the cylinders
would have been 28°. In the example as finally made tappet adjustment was effected by inserting shims of known thickness between the
tappet and valve stem, using a design of lazy-tongs made up for
the job. It sounds complicated, but inserting a shim against the stop-
watch required only five minutes for the eight tappets.

The induction pipe was cast in the crankcase and the ducts or leads
to the inlet valves were cored in the cylinder castings, quite an unusual feature. When first run the firing was found to be rather uneven

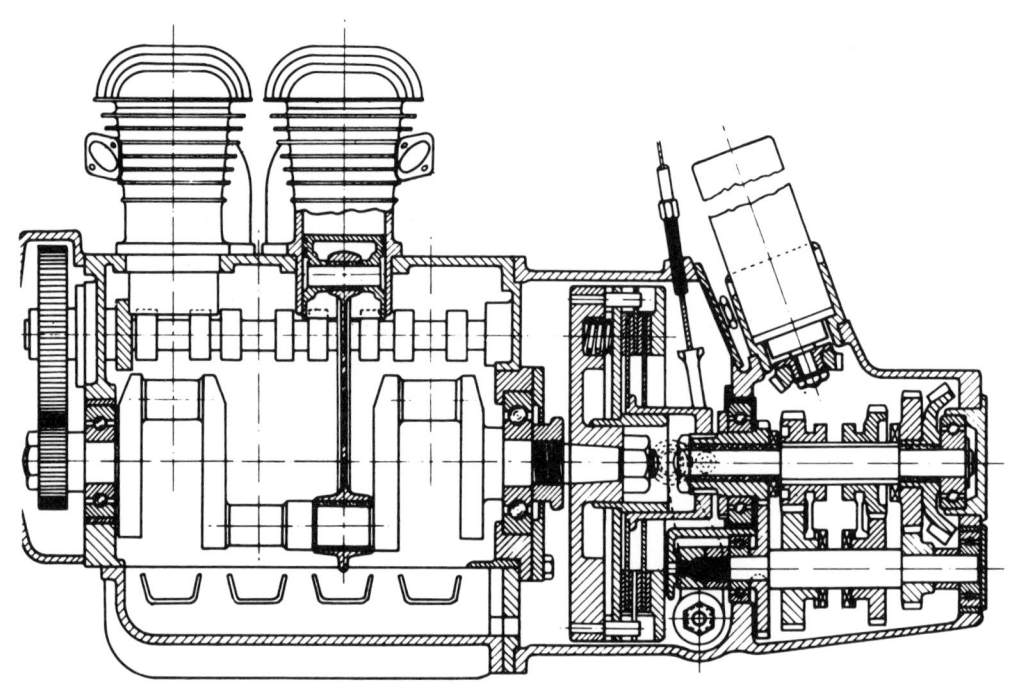

LONGITUDINAL SECTION

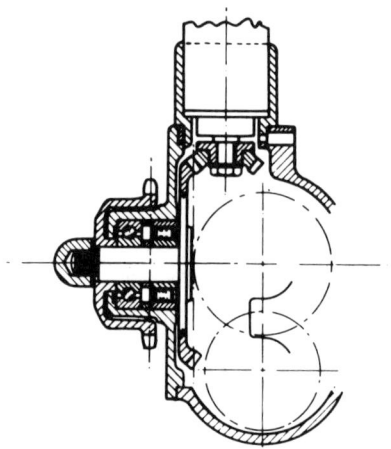

TRANSVERSE VIEW ON FINAL BEVEL DRIVE

34   *Some further details of the Vee Four*

35 The Brough Superior Straight Four

so another crankshaft costing £85 was fitted making a great improvement. It was not the maker's intention to market it until later in 1928 after a further series of tests and checks had been made. Designed and produced by George Brough, the working drawings had been made by (the late) Isaac Cohen. When on show at Olympia it was protected in a large glass case in turn protected by three large policemen. Its price tag was £250. Cooling however was found at times to be a trifle uneven.

Probably no other maker ever achieved the production of two different four-cylinder machines in two consecutive years but such

36 A second view of the Straight Four

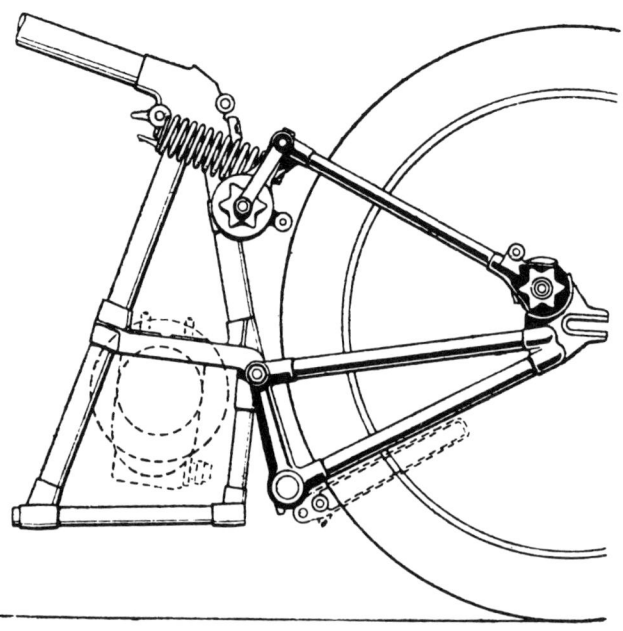

37   Diagram of the Draper spring frame

was the case at Haydn Road, for in 1928 there came the Straight Four depicted in all its glory in Figs. 35 and 36. Fancy, two new 'fours' at a period when the hysterical hero worship accorded the single-cylinder engine had to be experienced to be believed. At a period, too, at least twenty years after the single cylinder had died a languishing death in motor-cars and in other branches of mechanical engineering; and where it was still to be found (apart from small agricultural units) it was usually a double-acting steam engine with therefore two crank efforts per revolution.

In this new Straight Four the cylinders were 57 × 80 mm., 900 c.c., using a compression ratio of 5·1 to 1. Running in three bearings the crankshaft of nickel-chrome steel was bored for lightness and for lubrication, the oil being circulated under pressure to all necessary parts by a mechanical pump. In the train of gears operating the cam-shaft was inserted an idler pinion of Textolite to ensure silent running and another train of gears also drove the dynamo. Of integral construction with the rear end of the engine was the gearbox containing three speeds, there being a reduction of 2 to 1 in the final bevel drive to the rear-chain driving-sprocket. The speedometer also was driven from the gearbox, and the clutch was of the single-plate type lined with friction surface material and running in oil. A rather unusual tyre section was preferred in this instance, viz. 27″ × 4″, wired on, the brake drums being 8″ inside diameter. With the black cylinder finning and polished ribbed aluminium exhaust manifold it was a combination to charm the eye of the aesthete and the engineer alike. The engine was built by our friends Motosacoche à Genève to George Brough's designs and he was greatly helped by W. D. Marchant, sometime technical adviser to this firm.

This elegant machine like the A.G.S. could be fitted with the Draper patent sprung frame illustrated in Fig. 37, and in the Frontispiece, from which the action of the mechanism is, I think, quite obvious. Both top and bottom pivots were in long bearings adjustable by right-handed screws, the movement of the rear axle being controlled by the twin coil springs beneath the saddle. As the pivot bearings were long any side play at the rear spindle was negligible. If desired the compression coils could be enclosed within tubular plated sliding covers. The motor-cycling press welcomed it and said: 'It can be said that to apply the phrase "poetry of motion" to this mechanism is not to make use of a mere platitude but to state something that is very near the truth.'

This delightful device was protected by Patent No. 259,401 in the name of Alick Darby Draper, and a list of Mr Draper's patents will be found in the appropriate appendix.

CHAPTER V

The Largest, the Smallest and another Four

During this time all types had been favourably received by the motor-cycling public and its press, among which the o.h.v. 680 had been made in goodly numbers, but retaining the rigid frame. What about installing the o.h.v. 680 engine in a spring frame and allied with some other distinctive feature?, thought the Haydn Road brains trust. The answer was to finish off such a combination of engine and frame with an all-black eggshell finish and call it the *Black Alpine 680*, which can be seen in Fig. 38, having been first exhibited at the 1929 Show. Although the famous bulbous-nosed saddle tank was now all black, the narrow silver or gold-leaf line is still retained so that the tank 'gives the Machine a particularly dignified appearance'. Whereas the o.h.v. 680 had by now a foot change mounted on the gearbox, a hand change was retained on the *Black Alpine*, as may be seen from the illustration, but in each model the solo gear ratios were 4·5, 5·4, 7·49 and 13 to 1. Quick changes by hand were more of a knack soon acquired than anything else and many readers and owners may have obtained top by moving the lever but with the engine allowed to turn over fairly fast. For over-taking hesitant motor-cars this third gear was a boon.

38 *The* Black Alpine

39   A later and modified version of the o.h.v. 680

In 1931 a slightly modified o.h.v. 680 was made available, seen in Fig. 39, wherein will be noted the now enclosed rocker gear, quite different from the original in Fig. 28, but which we have noted already in the detail in Fig. 29, the date of this alteration being November 1928 as I mentioned previously.

Early in 1928 an o.h.v. 680 engine was seized at random from among those in stock at Haydn Road, taken back to Tottenham and subjected to a severe test under an independent observer.

It was a run for two 10-hour tests followed by six 5-hour tests making 50 hours in all at a continuous speed of 3,000 r.p.m., the throttle of the Binks carburettor being set half-open. Average output was 13·62 b.h.p., equivalent to 3,000 miles at 55 m.p.h. with a sidecar on Shell No. 1 petrol using a compression ratio of 5½ to 1. Consumption of oil and fuel was found to be 858·3 and 54 m.p.g. respectively. Upon dismantling after the test no wear or other marks were to be found on any parts, no carbon was visible on the heads and ports and what little carbon there was on the pistons was removed with the fingernail. Afterwards the engine was carefully re-assembled and road tested when it averaged 82½ m.p.h. over the measured quarter-mile.

680 c.c. was in those days a popular capacity but not every rider desired an overhead valve machine, and towards the end of 1926 a side-valve version of the o.h.v. 680 was available utilising the old Mark I frame and fittings and known as the s.v. 680.

40 Front side view of the s.v. 680, sometimes called the Brough Superior Junior and made for 1933 only

A derivative from the ordinary s.v. 680 was the 5–15 model, one of which left the works on 17 April 1927 having engine No. 73738 by J. A. Prestwich and frame No. 847 of the short type. Here, as in the traction-engine world, dates and numbers can be misleading because although another 5–15 with frame No. 877 was delivered on 15 June 1929 another with an earlier frame No. 866 left the works as late as June 1932. Although without so much sheer punch as its o.h.v. counterpart this s.v. machine was a most charming bicycle to ride. Listed at £65 fully equipped it was a bargain, although at this price the much more expensive Castle forks could not be included. In order therefore to make it within reach of a wider public the 5–15 had an open diamond frame and a front-end view of one is to be seen in Fig. 40. It had an extra refinement however of the magdyno shield, being carried beneath the crankcase to the lowest cross bolt. Three speeds were incorporated in the Sturmey-Archer gearbox, the pinions therein being formed from 120-ton steel, and change was made by hand lever. A particularly interesting feature was a cast aluminium port between the cylinder and tailpipe, clearly seen in Fig. 40, which promoted silence and provided cool running. In Fig. 41 will be noticed an offside view of this delectable little machine showing an alternative exhaust system with both pipes on the same side, and without the extended magdyno shield. Over 200 were built and many were exported to Vienna incidentally, Eddy Meyer being the agent.

A leaflet was published dealing only with this delightful model

41 Offside view of the delectable s.v. 680, also known as the 5/15 which previously was made first c1926

and the concluding remarks by the maker were: 'It glides along in almost perfect silence! It starts by merely depressing the starter pedal. It will do 75 miles per hour if necessary, 80 miles to the gallon of petrol, and 1,000 per gallon of lubricating oil.' Cheap and luxurious transport with No. 1 petrol at 1s. 5½d. per gallon—a joy the present generation will, unfortunately, never know!

Such a charming engine is I feel worthy of a drawing, and the original of that reproduced in Fig. 42 is dated 24 June 1926. Having a bore and stroke of 70×88 mm. it had the crankcase internals similar to its overhead valve counterpart and in many instances Prestwich's own oil pump could be fitted in place of a Pilgrim. The plugs are screwed into the inlet valve caps and the compression taps into the side of the undetachable heads, following the practice in the 1,000 c.c. engine. The remaining features in the drawings are, I think, self-explanatory. Of the two models that in Fig. 41 was the earlier.

If 680 c.c. was a popular capacity in the 1930's then 500 c.c. was particularly common, fathered no doubt by this latter figure being the maximum permissible for most ordinary racing. Almost every maker in the motor-cycling world produced a 'five hundred' of some sort, and therefore it is not surprising George gave this size his attention so that the first 'baby' of the Brough Superior range, as it has been called, was despatched on 24 January 1931. The J.A.P. engine, No. PTOC/H 8445/S, had cylinders 62·5×80 mm., 498 c.c., its general design being based upon the T.T. engine raced in the Isle of Man in 1930. With a racing compression ratio this engine would propel a machine in excess of 90 m.p.h., but with the touring ratio of

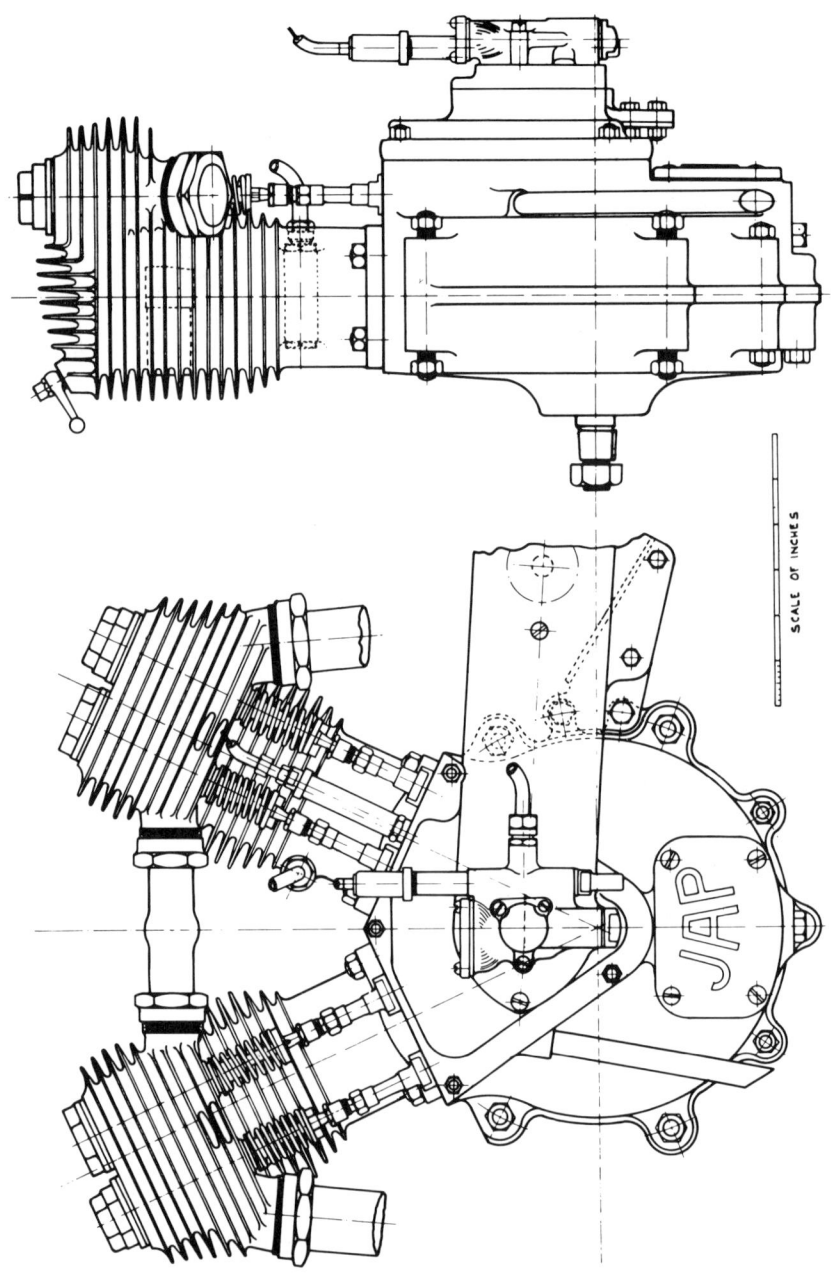

SCALE OF INCHES

42   *Drawing of the 680 s.v. J.A.P. engine*

43 Baby of the Brough Superior range—the o.h.v. 500

7 to 1 using 50/50 Shell-Benzole mixture 84 m.p.h. was attained in top and 75 m.p.h. in third gear, the four ratios in the Sturmey-Archer box being 4·9, 5·9, 10·6 and 13·8 to 1. In Fig. 43 Castle forks are fitted although originally 'Monarch' forks, sometimes designated 'Castle-Brampton' were used on a prototype. Both types gave a rock steady ride all through the speed range.

List price of the o.h.v. 500 was 100 guineas rigid frame only, a fairly high figure for a five-hundred at this time, but it was the maker's intention that the owner could by dismantling road accoutrements and withdrawing compression plates, quickly modify it for racing purposes or as the manufacturer stated 'this machine is convertible to a "pukka" racing machine quite easily by the owner'. Apart from the engine the remaining specification was identical to the contemporary o.h.v. 680. Of the o.h.v. 500, nine examples left the works in 1931, three of which are now preserved and hugely treasured

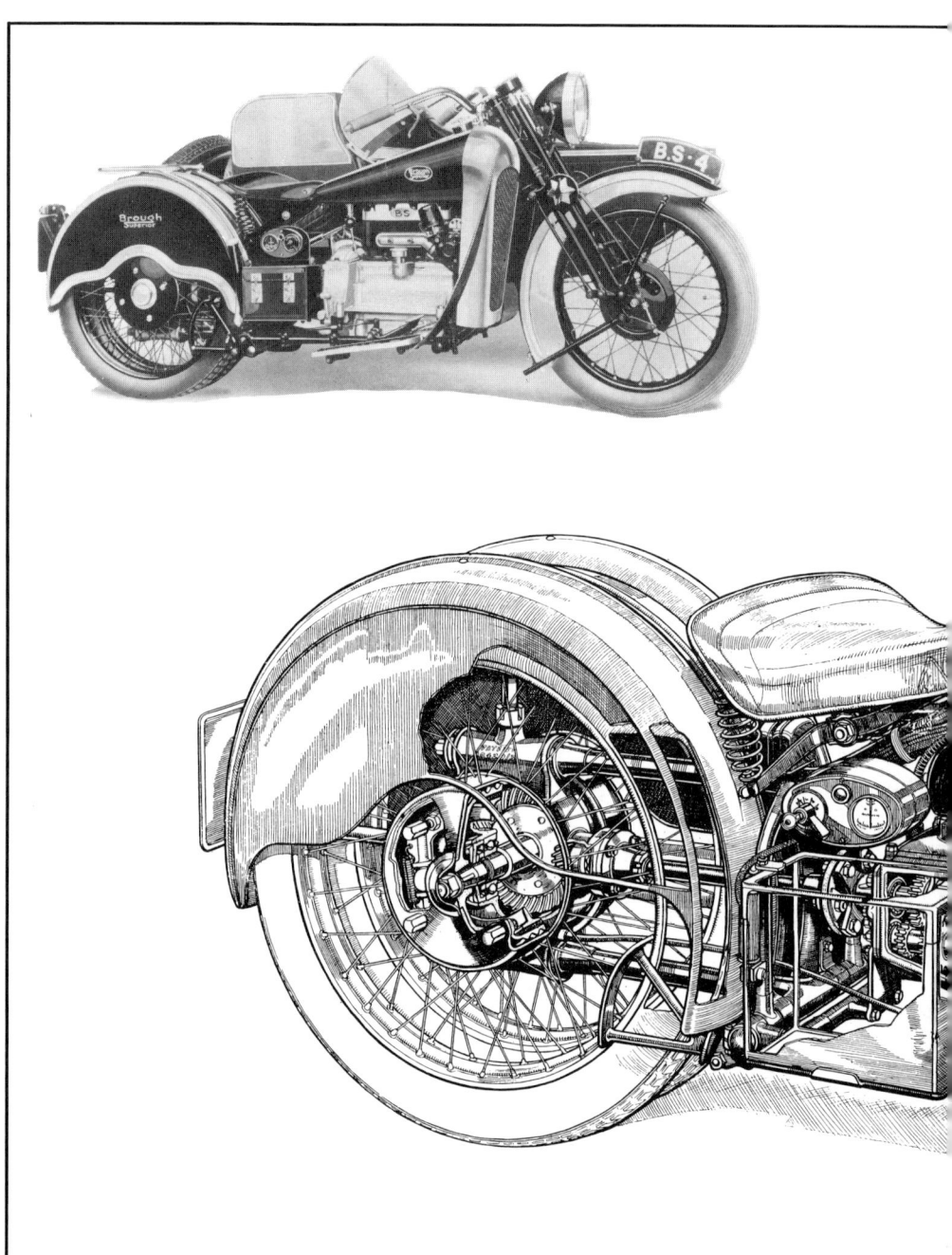

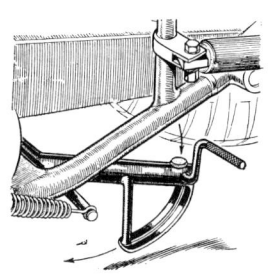

left: 44   A regal machine—
the 800 c.c. Four Cylinder

below: 45   Diagrammatic
details of the 800 c.c. Four

46 *Rear-wheel details of the machine in Fig. 44*

by their owners. The detail in Fig. 29 we must remember shows the enclosure of the pushrods and rockers on the o.h.v. 500 engine. Often in the past so-called knowledgeable people have flatly disbelieved a five-hundred Brough Superior was ever made and I hope they are now enlightened.

This year, 1931, was outstanding in the activities at Haydn Road for another reason, viz. the design and production of yet another 'four', seen in all its regality in Fig. 44. What a departure from stilted, stereotyped, standard single-cylinder practice this was! A job to gladden the mind of the particular rider and engineer, it could only have been conceived and produced in a factory uncluttered by the conventions of that time.

Dealing with the engine first. This was an Austin Seven four, but having a bore and stroke of 57·9 × 76 mm. giving a capacity of 800 c.c. and with an output of 23 b.h.p. at 4,600 r.p.m. There were too a few special parts included. Its capacity was therefore a little more than that used in the car engine. A detailed examination of Fig. 45 reveals a single camshaft to operate all valves, a two-bearing crankshaft balanced both statically and dynamically. The cylinders are cast in one block and to enhance the balance still further all connecting rods were machine finished. Fitted to the cylinder block was the aluminium head which, with the tank removed, could be dismantled clear of the top frame tube. In this application of this famous engine a single-lever special Amal carburettor was mounted on the nearside as were the inlet and exhaust manifolds. Skew gears drove the dynamo across the front of the engine together with the distributor and contact-breaker gear.

Naturally the familiar bulbous-nosed saddle tank is retained with twin film-type radiators extended upwards to merge with the curve of the nose of the tank. Splayed either side are the legshields developed to a parabola at their outside edge as may be seen also in Fig. 44.

Coming now to the transmission this is via the car-type box and single dry-plate clutch bolted directly to the rear of the crankcase. Four gears were incorporated in this box one of which was a reverse, most handy when manoeuvring a heavy outfit but not without its humorous side when handled by a novice! The forward ratios were 5, 7·1 and 12·7 to 1 with the lever and selector mechanism mounted on the lid of the box. But to prevent unintentional use of the reverse gear, a Haydn Road-made trigger and cam were added to the gate, so shaped that it aided movement of the lever from first to second gears. In place of the usual kick starter we have an electric starter, the motor being placed slightly above and parallel to the line of the box.

Following the transmission still further back, the drive from the rear of the box was via a flexible coupling to a propeller shaft having cut solid on it at the extreme end a high-tensile bevel pinion engaging with a mating crown wheel. The short cross-shaft carrying this crown wheel had a rear road wheel mounted on each end of it clearly seen in the photograph in Fig. 46. As the centres of the twin rear wheels were less than 18″ the vehicle remained—in law—a motor cycle. The idea of twin rear wheels had been tried way back in 1906 when the Rex concern produced a solo with two tyres on the same rear wheel, the rims being 2″ apart. In this instance the idea was patented and road holding was said to be very good when tested. Little more was heard of the arrangement and so it was not until twenty-eight years later that the idea was put again to good use. Exhaust was by a single tail pipe and fishtail on the nearside.

To house such an engine the base of the frame was made in the form of a cross-braced rectangle terminating at its rear end in a form of Gothic arch and from the apex of the arch and the middle of its base there were continued rearwards the two tubes seen in Fig. 45, on which were mounted the rear right-angled bevel-drive box. In front was a single heavy down tube divided near the bottom to clear the end of the crankcase. Extra-heavy Castle forks completed the main specification.

There were, as usual, a few refinements. A 42-ampere-hour accumulator, for example, ignition and lighting switches beneath the saddle and out of the way of impish urchins, the starter knob under the tank. Note too the deep valancing round the rear wheels—a refinement hailed with quivering delight as something new only a year or so ago! With such a mounting for the rear wheels, they were obviously made quickly detachable with a powerful 8″ brake in one hub. Picture the fine black finish, the striking effect of the twin radiators and chrome tank front end and the graceful curves and lines worked into the legshields, windscreen and valances.

A few main dimensions here might not be out of place. Wheelbase, 59½″, saddle height 25″, ground clearance 6½″, tank capacity 3½ gallons, sump capacity 7 pints of oil. Consumption was 50 m.p.g. at speeds of 50/55 m.p.h. and 2,500 m.p.g. of oil. Rear tyres were each 26″ × 3″ and front 26″ × 3·5″. Priced at £188 complete with cruiser sidecar to match.

Altogether ten examples of this original design left the works, the first on 15 January 1932 and another on 20 March 1932 with engine No. 131039/M, the last being completed in 1934. There are still several in working order owned by enthusiasts and giving excellent service. One had girder forks.

There remains the matter of the new design of centre-rolling spring-up stand fitted to this water-cooled straight four, and seen in the inset detail in Fig. 45. It was based on Patent No. 26429 of 1931 and in brief the principle employed was not to make the centre of the curved foot coincidental with the centre of the pivot—it is therefore part of the circumference of an ellipse. In pressing down the stand it rolls from the minimum radius on to its maximum radius the rise being therefore the difference between the two radii. Very simple and the kind of thing one wonders why one did not think of oneself!

Two years later in·1933 came yet another machine, having the largest capacity—1096 c.c.—of any of the range so far, the cylinders being 85·7 × 95 mm. Of J.A.P. manufacture, it was specially produced for the Brough Superior range with the cylinders at an included angle of 60° instead of the usual 50°, thus giving a more even torque and consequently smoother running. Its other main features were dry-sump lubrication, totally enclosed side valves, quickly detachable heads, bevel-driven magdyno, polished ports and roller big-end

47   *The 11–50 Special*

bearings. It was quite happy hauling a heavy sidecar up to 75 m.p.h.
or, with solo gears and Castle instead of Monarch forks, attaining
more than 90 m.p.h. In fact, one model upon which extra skill was
exercised during erection reached 101 m.p.h.! The gear ratios adopted
in this example, viz. 3·75, 4·75, 6·5 and 10 to 1 respectively represent
6,066 r.p.m. at 101 m.p.h.—and this from a despised side-valve,
remember! For more ordinary uses the suggested ratios were 4·2,
4·83, 6·13 and 10·59 to 1, but greater smoothness resulted from the
former series at high speeds. The same may be said of the opposite
end of the scale—12 m.p.h. in top requiring a mere 760 r.p.m. A
flexibility suggesting a steam engine one might say. A prototype had
been in action sometime during 1932.

What of the consumption of such a large engine? Over give-and-
take roads 60 m.p.g. of petrol and 2,000 of oil. And the road holding?
As *Motor Cycling* wrote: 'The Castle forks swallow up end shocks
like magic. Most remarkable of all, perhaps, is the freedom from fore
and aft pitching in cornering on indifferent surfaces at high speed.
Nor is it the comparatively heavy weight of the big twin which is
wholly responsible for this most striking virtue.' Upon which it is
most instructive and enlightening to ruminate that today we are led
to believe (if we are sufficiently absorbent) that the sliding tubular
fork is the acme of excellence. That being so then those quoted words
are wrong, but knowing the Brough Superior and Castle forks as I
and many others do—then it is the fork of today which must be
suspect. One cannot have it both ways! I much surmise it to be not so
much a matter of pre-war products being out of date as cheapness of
manufacture in today's goods.

The side valves are enclosed in tubular covers split vertically, and by removing the front half the tappets were immediately accessible, similar to the system used on the SS80 as can be seen in a glance at Fig. 55.

Both wheels were 27″ diameter fitted with a 4″ rear and a 3·5″ front tyre and both brakes were 8″ diameter. Listed at £99 12s. 6d., it was fully equipped, and such value for money has never been surpassed post-war.

A year or so later a few modifications had been carried out as experience had dictated and in 1934 the revised version was designated the 11–50 Special. A general view of one is to be seen in Fig. 47 when it will be noted the magdyno is now chain-driven, and the side valves are now enclosed by neat part-plain, part-ribbed alloy covers seen clearly in the more detailed picture reproduced in Fig. 48 which, incidentally, illustrates the extremely high standard of finish. In this case the compression ratio was 5 to 1. To obviate distribution difficulties a novel and modified Amal carburettor was fitted comprising one float chamber serving two mixing chambers, the assembly being flanged and bolted to the middle of a divided induction pipe as will be seen in the further detail in Fig. 49. Each unit was adjusted and tuned separately thus producing even carburation and therefore even firing.

Complete with sidecar and passenger the outfit scaled 7 cwt. 1 qr. 2 lb. and on test the maximum speed recorded with this load was 72 m.p.h. in top gear, 68 in third and 60 in second gear, the equivalent engine speeds being 4,430, 5,120 and 5,390 r.p.m. respectively.

Although designed essentially as a solo bicycle, certain customers did require a sidecar to be fitted to an 11–50 Special but there is a limit to the speed at which one can corner with a combination. To facilitate left-hand cornering the proprietor at Haydn Road produced in 1933 his famous banking sidecar, of which the technical details can be gleaned from the perspective views depicted in Fig. 50. The wheel proper is made in the form of a helix open at each end, and the wheel runs on an axle mounted on the arm A pivoted in the chassis at B. A plate riveted to the arm A has the hole C drilled in it, into which engages the plunger D, this plunger being connected with a second plunger E. Therefore the control for both D and E is the Bowden cable F operated by the rider through the pedal and trigger gear G. Note both plungers are spring-loaded. H is a spring-loaded oil dashpot to damp downward movement (5½″) of the sidecar body. On a normal straight road the plunger D is in the hole C. Now let us

above: 48 A
detail of the
11–50

left:
49 Induction
details on the
11–50

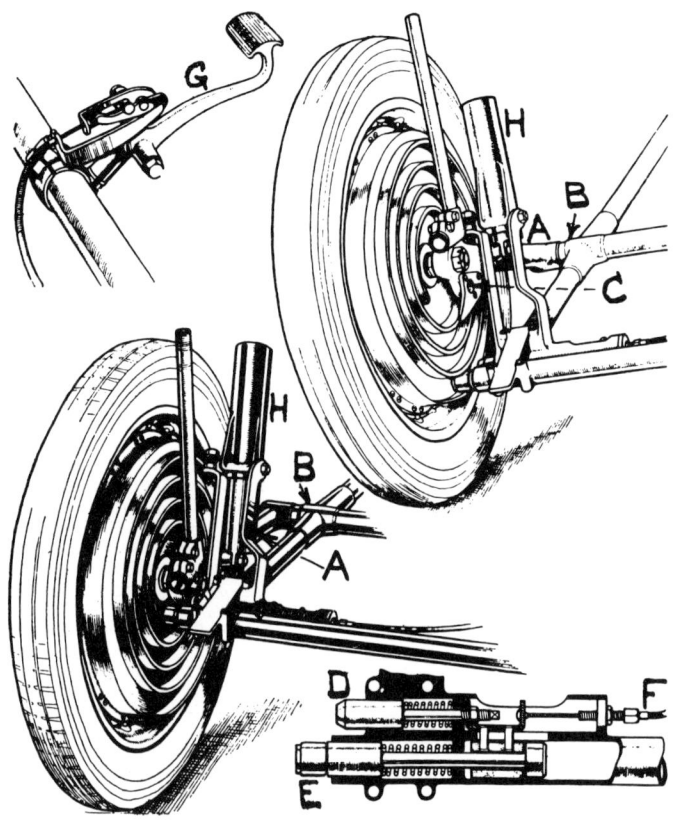

50 *George Brough's banking sidecar*

come to a left-hand corner. The rider withdraws D from the hole C when the body and passenger drops slowly to counteract the centrifugal force due to the curve. Upon the curve being negotiated and a little before 'pulling out of it', the trigger gear is released again when immediately E enters the outside end of the helix and with a few revolutions of the road wheel the body is returned to the normal horizontal position and the plunger D clicks into its hole C, thus again locking the mechanism.

I am told by several authorities that great speed and skill could be developed and corners taken at a velocity hitherto impossible. Like all excellent ideas it is so simple. I once asked George how he thought of it. 'I got the idea from the scroll in a self-centring chuck' came the devastating answer!

CHAPTER VI

SS100 and SS80 Redesigned, the Transverse 1,000 and the *Dream*

Simultaneously with the improvement of the 11–50 into the 11–50 Special, comparable changes were being made to the SS100 and SS80 so that in November 1933 there was shown the New SS100 illustrated in Fig. 51.

The principal new feature was the redesigned J.A.P. engine seen in detail in the sectional drawing reproduced in Fig. 52. Having a bore and stroke of 80×99 mm., 996 c.c., it was classified as the 8–75 and developed 74 b.h.p. at 6,200 r.p.m. with a compression ratio of 8 to 1. The upper seatings of the crankcase to receive the cylinders are raised some little distance more than formerly, permitting both cylinders to be deeply spigoted for about one-third of their length below the neck flanges into the crankcase, thus ensuring great rigidity and freedom from vibration. It suggested great compactness when,

51   The new SS100

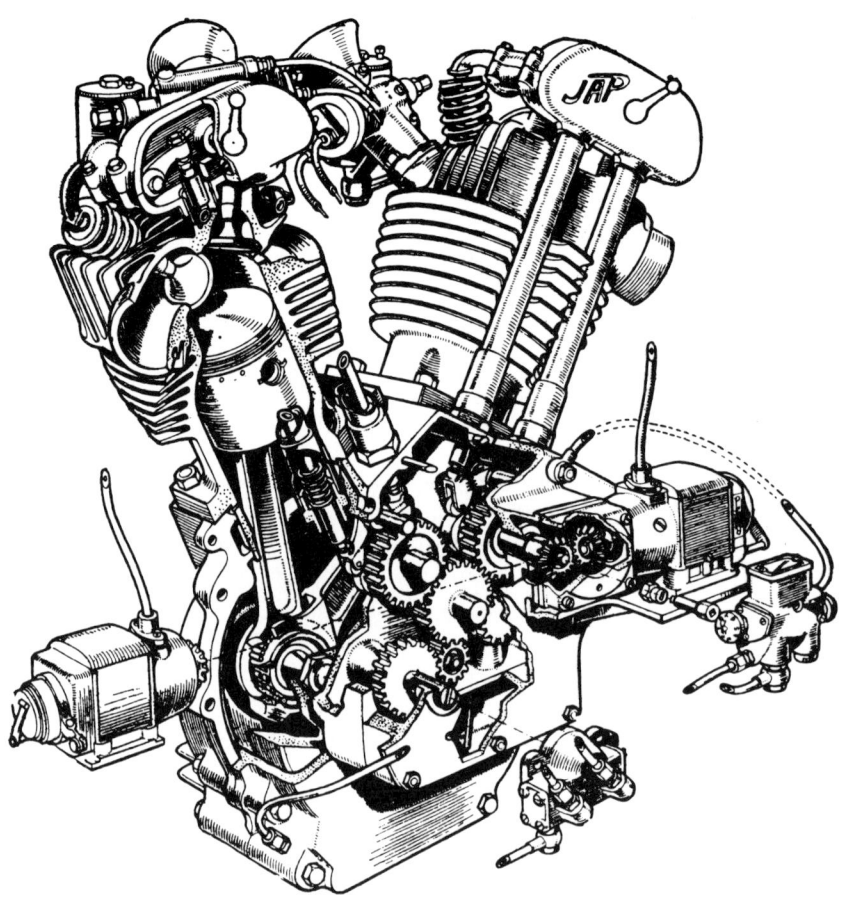

52 *Details of the new SS100 engine*

in Fig. 51, it was seen mounted in the frame. Whereas in the 11–50 engine a carburettor having one float chamber but two mixing chambers and a divided induction pipe was used, in the New SS100 twin separate carburettors and twin magnetos (one a magdyno naturally) were preferred. It had been intended to participate in the 1933 Sidecar T.T. and this new engine was devised for this purpose but unfortunately the event never took place. Steel was used for the flywheels, but further details such as the caged roller bearings to each connecting rod big end are clearly seen in the drawing. Dry-sump lubrication was entrusted not to one but to four pumps, one double pump driven from the train of timing gears feeding the big ends and timing gear, its other half scavenging the sump and returning the oil to the tank. Another double or duplex pump driven from the magneto bevels feeds half of it to one cylinder and the other half to the other cylinder, the lubricant being fed to the cylinders through a series of holes in the cylinder walls and through an annular space between the walls of the cylinders and the deeply spigoted crankcase.

Four ratios were arranged in the Sturmey-Archer box, both wheels had 27″ × 4″ tyres, the down tube of the frame was 1½″ diameter and of 8 s.w.g., and there were the Castle forks.

It is here with every regret that one has to record the death of W. E. Brough which occurred on 11 December 1934, when he was in his seventy-third year. Since producing the last horizontally opposed Brough twin in 1925 he had specialised not only in the reconditioning of engines of all types but in particular repairs covering cylinder boring and honing, sleeving, crankshaft grinding, re-metalling of bearings, valve re-seating, starter rings and general engineering. He was also one of the main distributors for Specialloid pistons. As one would guess successfully, George succeeded to the Vernon Road Works and property and from 1935 onwards a move was made by degrees from Haydn Road so that ultimately the Brough Superior came to be made where the Brough had been years before. It is perhaps the only example in the motor-cycling world of the products of a son being continued in the works of his father.

53   An SS100 with hairpin valve springs

54 Further details of the engine in Fig. 53

It meant memorising the new postal address (the telegraphic remained the same), but this the enthusiasts did in their stride as they had done the original address fifteen years earlier!

Towards the end of 1935 an alternative engine by A.M.C. Ltd of Plumstead, Kent could be fitted. Pictured in Fig. 53 it has in company with the Frontispiece perhaps the finest 'lines' of any comparable solo 'Thousand' ever made and the eye, roving from the top of the rear mudguard, along the saddle and tank top to the bars, is charmed. It is certainly a confirmation of the engineering truth that usually if a piece of mechanism looks right, it is right. In fact, it looks so right that it would be difficult to fault the position of any item. They all blend, one with and complementary to another. I am not antagonistic to genuine mechanical progress but I venture to say it would need but the intrusion and infliction of a dual seat or sliding tubular forks upon it to ruin the masterpiece. If left alone its lines will never become dated. I have the originals of the Frontispiece and Fig. 53 on my study wall keeping company a Rolls Royce of steam road locomotives from a famous Norfolk works, and these three never fail to inspire me and gladden my eye.

Here we have an engine, outlined in Fig. 54, with hairpin valve springs and a bore and stroke of 85·5 × 85·5 mm. with the cylinder

55 *Enclosure of valves on the SS80*

angle remaining at 50°. Other brief main particulars are both crank-shaft and mainshaft $1\frac{1}{2}''$ diameter running in a phosphor-bronze bearing to the timing and a three-row roller to the driving side. To obviate any transverse forces the front connecting rod was forked as was the maker's stipulation for every engine since 1919, the big-end bearing having four rows of rollers. Gudgeon pins in the Lo-Ex pistons were fully floating and ran in duralumin bushes. In the gear-box there were again four ratios, 3·5, 4·4, 6·7 and 11 to 1. With a compression ratio of only 6·5 to 1 an easy top speed of 102 m.p.h. could be attained, but for racing purposes the ratio was altered to 8 to 1. Such a machine craved to be driven hard, and in solo trim with speeds in the eighties where possible, the petrol consumption worked out at a little more than 51 m.p.g. Obviously with gentler driving it could be improved to nearer 70 m.p.g. Simultaneously the oil required was one pint in 325 miles or 2,600 m.p.g.!

As in the case of the 11–50 a carburettor with twin chambers and divided induction pipe was first used in this design, but in subsequent examples a single chamber fed by two float chambers was preferred, as illustrated in the enlarged detail in Fig. 54. Further comments I feel are superfluous and to suggest it is a picture full of appeal is merely to labour the obvious.

56 *The new SS80 of 1933*

Here it is opportune to bestow some further attention on the popular and proven SS80, which had remained somewhat unaltered from the example shown in Fig. 22. For 1928, however, the makers of the big side-valve engine decided, on George's suggestion, to enclose the valves, and this was accomplished by the simple yet effective method depicted in Fig. 55 using tubular covers split in halves vertically, and restrained in position by a spring. By a dexterous twist of the finger and thumb the front half could be detached and drawn away as seen in the photograph, which incidentally shows several later innovations made since that in Fig. 22 was designed—the compression springs of the spring frame, portions of the Castle forks, enclosed saddle springs and the exhaust system with one pipe each side. Hand-gear change was employed, the Sturmey-Archer heavyweight box containing four ratios of 4·5, 5·4, 7·9 and 13 to 1 in solo trim.

This design remained very much as seen in Fig. 55 for several years until in 1933 there was listed the first New SS80 to be seen in Fig. 56, having in this instance a rigid frame. Piquantly the maker wrote about it: 'Entirely redesigned—shorter and lower, with larger tanks and greater ground clearance—the size of a 350, the weight of a 500 and the performance of a . . . SS80.' Again the engine has the quickly detachable tubular valve spring covers but the cylinders now have only six fins above the covers instead of eleven as before, the aluminium ribbed exhaust pockets being retained. Where however a spring frame was specified the pipes were arranged one on each side as in Fig. 55. Gear ratios remained unchanged.

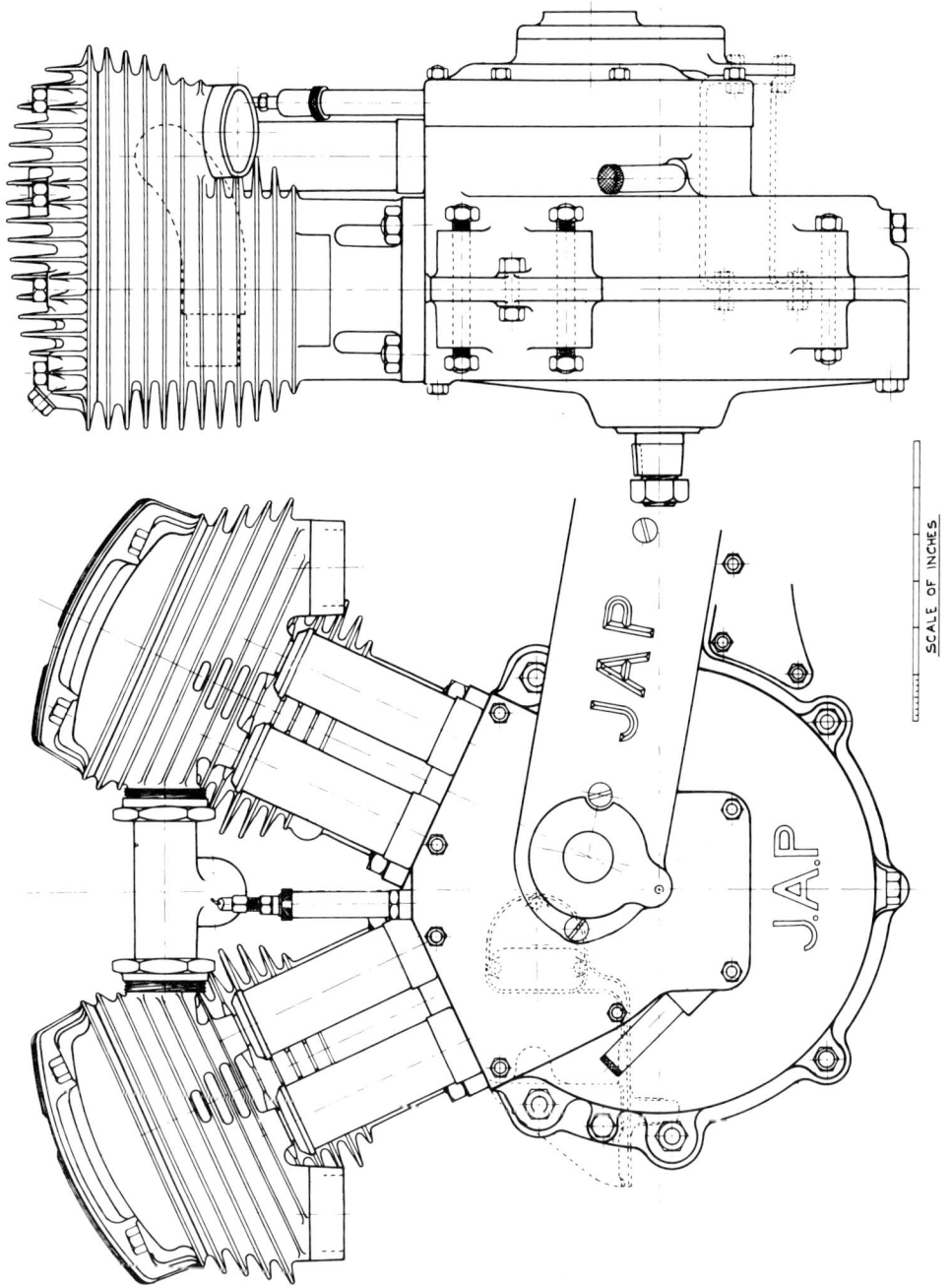

SCALE OF INCHES

57   Two outside views of the new SS80 engine

58   An SS80 Special

Two outside views in Fig. 57 provide further details of the new SS80 engine. It is scarcely necessary to point out the obvious modifications. But the heads are detachable, the plugs being screwed into the top, and only the familiar contours of the crankcase proclaim its descent from its illustrious progenitor seen a long time ago in Fig. 10.

Introduced after the 1934 Show and therefore first exhibited in 1935 was the SS80 Special shown in Fig. 58 powered now by another product of A.M.C. Ltd. Its cylinders were 85·5 × 85·5 mm., 990 c.c., with the cylinder angle still 50°, a three-cam timing gear with four-cam levers being incorporated in the timing chest. Lubrication was dry-sump, embodying a fabric filter in the oil tank beneath the saddle. Again the valves are totally enclosed but this time in a cavity forming part of the cylinder casting, both cavities being enclosed by a ribbed and inscribed alloy cover, each meeting its fellow on a vertical line, as may be seen from the photograph. Fig. 59 shows a sectioned view of this engine which I feel needs little further comment, the main features being quite clearly shown. Fig. 59 is Matchless design. B.S. had spade and forked rods and modified ports and angles. The valve-chest covers however are not Brough Superior but A.M.C. Standard. Note that in Fig. 58 a modified fork, the Brough-girder, perfected in the works, is fitted to this machine although Castle forks were obtainable at a slight extra cost. During the ensuing months it could be bought with a *de luxe* specification in which bottom-link forks were standard and twin synchronised carburettors, etc., the list price being £110, that for the Special being £95.

Towards the end of 1937 still further modifications were carried out on the valve cavities ensuring slightly better cooling, as will be seen from a glance at Fig. 60. Both cavities are less in height allowing for grease-nipple lubrication of the guides, the covers being now shallower, still inscribed but with fewer ribs.

Those with an eye for detail will have observed in Fig. 60 a new rear-wheel fixing of which an exploded line drawing is depicted in Fig. 61. Each rear-axle fork has a cylinder formed with it sliding inside another located in the top 'jaw' of the rear frame tubes, both cylinders being held in position by a long bolt passing through the

59   Sectional diagram of the A.M.C. SS80 engine

73

60 Further modifications to the SS80

strong compression spring. A smaller rebound spring will be seen just below the fork end cylinder and the lower 'jaw'. Utterly simple and straightforward and if kept filled with grease the device is good for 60,000 trouble-free miles as I have found. A more detailed view of the invention fitted to an SS100 can be enjoyed by studying Fig. 62 which again and additionally illustrates the very high standard of finish insisted upon by the maker. Rear-axle springing I might add is a really old problem having caused the builders of steam road vehicles much intense thought from *c.* 1865 onwards. Coil springs, laminated springs, spring spokes and spring hubs—all were patented, applied to engines and tried out. I will not whisper how indebted the modern spring hub of one famous make is to a certain traction engine! So it was with some real enthusiasm I once mentioned to the maker the simplicity of this new system of rear springing and remarked it was one of those things anyone might have thought of. 'Yes,' came the instant rejoinder, 'Why didn't you?' This time I countered with the words of Milton: 'Th' invention all admired, and each how he to be th' inventor missed, so easy it seemed once found, which yet unfound, most would have thought impossible.' George continued to smile.

At Olympia in 1937 the Brough Superior stand was again, I almost wrote 'as usual', one of the great centres of attraction, the centre-piece being the Transverse Twin illustrated in Fig. 63. Ever since the

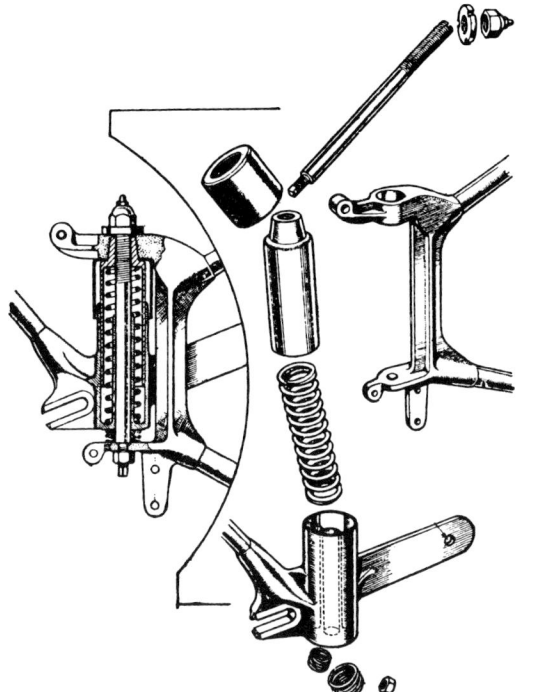

left: 61   Plunger-spring mounting for the rear axle

below: 62   The plunger springing as fitted to a late SS100

above: 63   The Transverse Twin of 1937

production of the Transverse Vee Four which has delighted us in Figs. 32, 33 and 34 the maker had the idea of a simpler and alternative layout using a standard side-valve engine. In this example the A.M.C. design now proved successfully in the New SS80 is used, but with the valve gear set forward and screened by the beautifully smooth oil tank. On the other side the extended crank or driving shaft carries a flywheel-type single-plate clutch, the appropriate crankcase half being suitably modified to match up with an Austin box containing four synchromesh ratios, clearly seen in the sectional view depicted in Fig. 64. One difficulty confronting any designer of a longitudinal transmission terminating in a right-angled drive is the mounting of a kick-starter crank. Venerable readers will remember it was attempted in the famous A.B.C. by fixing the pedal so that its travel was at right angles to the centre line of the bicycle. The same applies to the B.M.W. where it is on the nearside. In the Nottingham Transverse

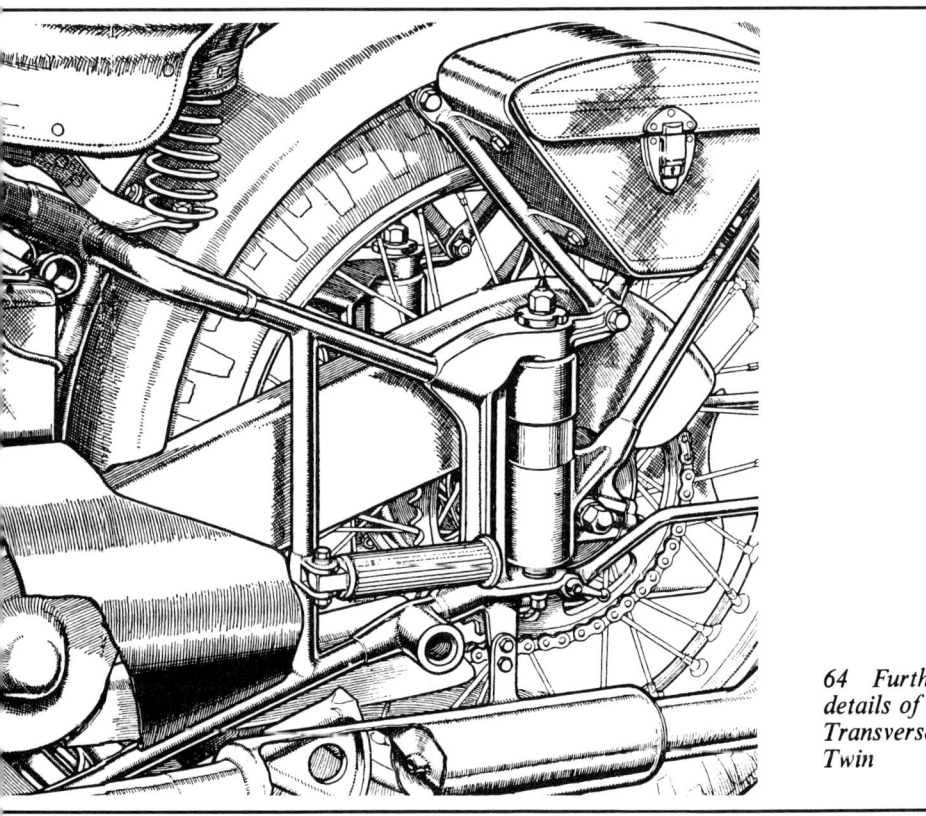

64 Further details of the Transverse Twin

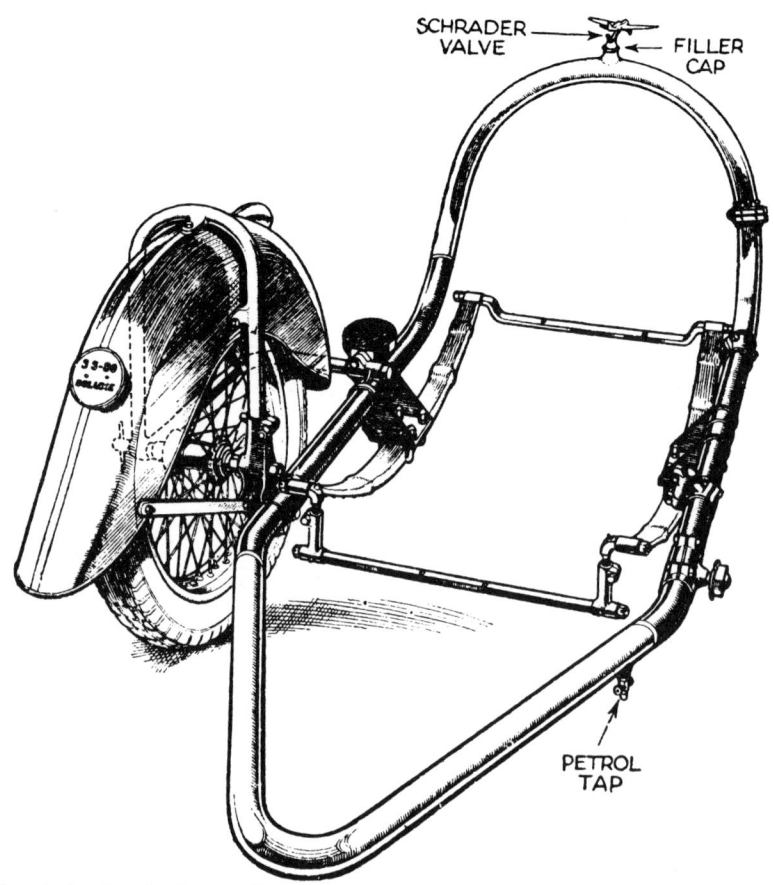

SCHRADER VALVE   FILLER CAP

PETROL TAP

65   A single-tube loop sidecar chassis

Twin however the problem was solved simply by providing a cross-shaft mounting on one end of the rear-chain driving-sprocket and on the other the kick-starter crank with the driven bevel wheel of the final bevel drive between them. Again quite simple and permitting the rider to kick-start in the orthodox manner. Combined and alternative hand and foot levers were provided for the clutch and a right-hand pedal for the foot gear-change. The lower tubes of the cradle frame had to be altered to house the new engine and gearbox fixing but the rest of the frame followed normal practice and incorporated the rear plunger springing, the front being taken care of by Monarch forks. Such an arrangement of cylinders allows an extremely simple exhaust system with the twin pipes low and parallel to the ground giving an impression of additional stability to the whole machine.

This famous bicycle had an engine number 4,000 BS/X, no number on the frame, and left the works on 27 August 1938, having been purchased by W. Douglas, Esq. Its registration number is FAU 85 and it is still in use in Scotland.

If we examine the entries in the M.C.C.'s Edinburgh Trial in 1936 we shall find George Brough entered on an SS80 and sidecar, and he went on to win a Premier Award. There was nothing unusual in this, of course, he'd been entering since 1908, but if there was anything unusual it was to be found in the chassis of the sidecar, of which a pictorial view is illustrated in Fig. 65. It was protected by Patent No. 413,239 of 12 July 1934 in the name of Adolf Felber, 39 Arndstrasse, Vienna, XII, Austria, and it was George who had the enterprise to embark upon its development construction in England. It will be seen that the main framing consists of one single $2\frac{1}{4}$"-diameter tube joined by a butt weld, and the length was so calculated that the volume of the tube equalled 2 gallons of petrol. By applying the tyre pump to the Schrader valve in the filler cap the contents could be forced out at the discharge tap at the bottom and led to the main tank through rubber tubing carried for this purpose. Such a loop frame is very strong, requiring no cross bracing, and therefore the body can be slung very low, the horizontal long semi-elliptical laminated springs giving a high degree of comfort. The stub axle is fixed to the left-hand side by a smaller tube or outrigger passing in front of the wheel and by a second vertical loop tube which also supports the mudguard, all clearly seen in Fig. 65. The four lugs for the four-point attachment to the bicycle are bolted to the tube eliminating brazing and consequent distortion due to local heating, and with a four-point fixing there is less liability to wring the bicycle frame.

Both sports and cruiser bodies could be fitted finished in black and red, and very imposing they looked. Known as the *Alpine Grand Sports Sidecar* and complete with super-sports body it was listed at £30 ex-works.

I suppose every enthusiastic yet thinking motor-cyclist has at some time or another turned over in his mind his ideal machine, a few probably putting their ideas on paper. Certainly many have bombarded the correspondence columns of the motor-cycling press over the years 'maintaining with no little heat their various opinions' as a famous dramatist puts it, but of all these ideal designs only a fortunate few ever get to the drawing-board stage, and of these occasionally a lone example of some 'dream' machine might be actually produced.

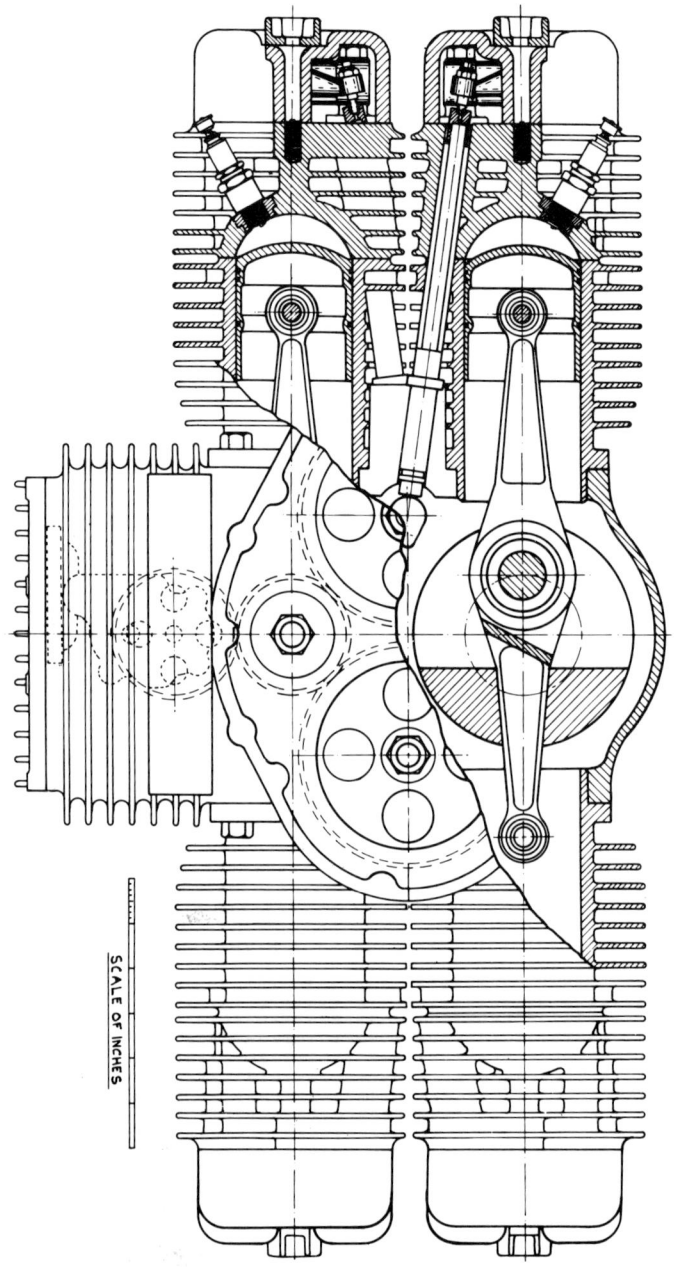

SCALE OF INCHES

66 First experimental Dream *engine*

One of these fortunate solitary examples was George Brough's *Dream* of 1938, the outcome of a triumvirate composed of the maker, F. Dixon and H. J. Hatch, the last-named then of Blackburnes, and it was in their drawing office that the new engine was first conceived. Hatch it may be remembered had been a designing draughtsman at J. A. Prestwich and Blackburnes and at one time was responsible for the Excelsior *Mechanical Marvel* which won the Lightweight T.T. in 1933, the 1935 Francis-Barnett *Stag* and later the triple o.h. camshaft 349 c.c. A.J.S. The *Dream*, like some previous examples, had four cylinders, but there all resemblance finishes for here we have the cylinders arranged after an H on its side or, if one prefers it, two horizontally opposed twins one above the other and geared together. Perfect balance was obtained by causing them to rotate in opposite directions but with each pair of pistons (when considered vertically), reciprocating together. George called it a 'flat vertical'—flat for balance, vertical for cooling.

As first designed the four cylinders were each 68 × 68 mm., 997 c.c., with the camshafts gear-driven, as can be followed from the general-arrangement drawing of the experimental engine in Fig. 66. Much development work was done on this engine and as might be expected many modifications resulted culminating in the second design detailed in the exploded view of Fig. 67, and it was this engine which was used in the first *Dream* exhibited at Olympia in 1938.

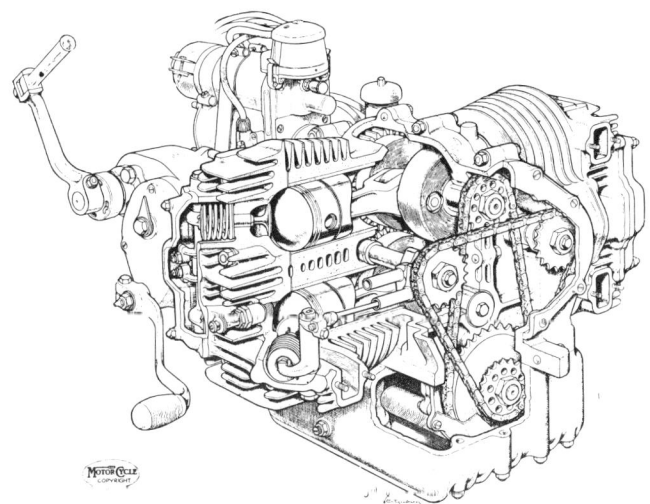

67   *Cut-away view of the* Dream *engine*

68　Outside rear view of the Dream *engine*

*69　Front
outside view
of the second
Dream engine*

The four cylinders were now 71×63 mm., 996 c.c., the domed pistons giving a compression ratio of 6·5 to 1. Noteworthy are the camshafts now chain-driven from the pumpshaft at the bottom, this in turn receiving its drive by another chain from the top crankshaft; the ratio of these chain drives being obviously 1 to 1 and 1 to 2 respectively. As in the prototype engine, the overhead valves are pushrod-and-rocker operated, the inlet cams on the rear ends and the exhaust cams on the front ends of the camshafts; the inlet valves incidentally were of somewhat larger diameter than the exhaust. This is because aspiration relies only on suction, whereas the exhaust exit is due to some force. Each pair of cylinders, i.e. right hand and left hand, had its Amal carburettor, and both were synchronised from a cross rod receiving its oscillation from the twist grip. Drive to the integrally constructed box was taken from the lower crankshaft through a twin-plate cork clutch on a flywheel spigoted to the shaft, through the gears and finally by a flexible coupling to the propeller shaft, the connection which can be seen in Fig. 68—showing an outside rear view of the engine. A front view is illustrated in Fig. 69 which shows the compact and neat outline. The rotation incidentally was anti-clockwise for the upper crankshaft when viewed from the front as in Fig. 69.

Final drive was by the propeller shaft already mentioned and an underslung worm and wormwheel on the rear axle, and even the propeller shaft was enclosed in a tube! As one would assume, the plunger rear-spring mounting was used, and variation in angularity of the propeller shaft under deflection of the axle was taken care of by the flexible coupling at the gearbox end; end variation due to the axle moving up and down in a vertical straight line and not radially about the gearbox as centre was permitted by the spigots seen in Fig. 68. In this way, no alteration in mesh of the worm and worm-wheel took place.

Ignition was by a Lucas magdyno and distributor specially made, driven at the rear and mounted on a platform in one with the top of the gearbox as will be noticed in Fig. 68. Note the width of the engine is only fractionally over 20″.

Lessons learnt in the past about exhaust-port cooling by external aluminium ports (compare Figs. 8, 22, 35 and 40) were applied to this engine, hence the neatly ribbed exhaust ports very evident in the picture of the complete machine shown in Fig. 70. Aluminium castings too were used for the carburettor mountings and to enclose the valves. Fig. 70 is extremely interesting, being a photograph taken

70 The complete Dream *before enamelling*

of the complete bicycle *before* enamelling and plating. Here it is opportune to state that every machine built at Haydn Road and later at Vernon Road was so assembled and everything made quite correct before dismantling. After plating and enamelling it was finally assembled, tested again and the lucky customer notified it was ready.

In the case of the *Golden Dream* the finish was the tint approximating closely to the colour of gorse when seen in the mass in blossom. It would have realised one of my fondest dreams to have parked a *Golden Dream* amongst the golden gorse locomotives of the Midland and Great Northern Joint Railway when in their heyday they too moved about the East Anglian countryside harmonising so effectively with the great expanses of gorse in bloom known probably to many of my readers.

But to return to the hard realities of mechanics. The connecting rods for example were one forked and the other bladed, the solid big ends running directly on the crankpins and there were no little-end bushes, the $\frac{5}{8}''$ gudgeon pins floating directly on the rod and in the pistons. Being solid the big-ends were fitted on the crankpins before bolting up together and balancing the crankshaft each in two halves, $1\frac{3}{8}''$ diameter, the width of the crankpin being $1\frac{3}{4}''$.

There are too a host of interesting small details. For instance the pushrods being short need be only $\frac{3}{16}''$ diameter of silver steel and they operated in short tunnels in their respective castings; the rocker spindles are drilled for oilways to lubricate the rockers which oscillate on the spindles, the last-named being stationary. Oil from the sump is forced through a Tecalemit filter and by registering grooves and holes through to the mainshaft and then the camshaft bearings. Oil for the big-ends travels to them through a hole in the flywheel boss and along a drilling in the shaft, it being remembered the whole system works under pressure. Besides the oil acting as a part coolant air can pass between the cylinders through the cavities cast in each block to be seen in Fig. 67.

Two gearboxes were procurable, one a three- and the other a four-speed, the former having an ordinary kick-starter pedal and the latter a hand lever to be pulled up smartly after the rider had comfortably seated himself in the saddle. There was no need to bother about a backfire because by a simple trigger arrangement the lever was instantly disconnected. These gearboxes, designed and made by the maker, were somewhat costly, the gears being cut by Messrs David Brown and Sons Ltd.

To remove the rear wheel it was only necessary to release the split caps holding the axle in the fork ends, disconnect the rear brake rod, lift the hinged portion of the mudguard and draw the whole rear drive and wheel away.

Some modifications to the ordinary frame had to be made and therefore one must note the widely splayed front down tubes and the original use of dual D section tubes connecting the saddle bracket to the rear cross stay, these tubes it will be seen are radiused to suit the curve of the mudguard. All joints incidentally were welded.

A few alterations were made to the Castle forks which were now wider to avoid 'pinching in' the front mudguard where it passes the tubes, and the most neat shock-absorbers. Gone are the twin parallel side rods actuated by the formerly extended bottom links and in their place is a short pin-jointed member connecting the front tube with the outer friction plate all clearly discernible in the photograph.

Another superiority was the toolbox formed in the space at the base of the tank where it saddles the top tube, the volume of the tank now increased to hold $4\frac{1}{2}$ gallons, and there was the 9"-diameter rear brake.

Quite apart from its original features this remarkable engine had one advantage over all the o.h.v. twins so far produced—the valves and springs (as in the side-valve engines) are now totally enclosed. It was the most original and outstanding attempt to break away from the lath and plaster of conventionalism in motor-cycles this country had, up to 1938, ever witnessed.

The price of the *Dream* had been fixed at £185 and four or five were produced during the early part of 1939 and one with the four-speed box was being erected for Olympia that year.

Then in September England was at war for the third time this century, and for the second time the productive capacity of the house of Brough applied to aid the war effort.

Up to the outbreak of hostilities from about 1935, we find production was concentrated upon three models only, the SS100, the SS80 and the 11–50 with the *Golden Dream* to be ordered specially. Thus two out of three standard machines were side-valves—an interesting point to consider when it is remembered the Brough Superior was supplied more to connoisseurs than to youthful speed merchants.

After September 1939 many orders were cancelled although a few deliveries were made. Many people have told me with the earnestness born of sincere conviction that this was not so but official records show the last SS100 with engine number 1106 BS/X2 left Vernon Road on 11 April 1940. The very last bicycle of all was an 11–50 delivered on 2 July that year.

CHAPTER VII

The Motor-Car

Popular rumour has it that so many admirers of the Brough Superior tackled the maker about producing a motor-car, that at last he decided to do so, but not without extensive aid and advice from F. Dixon and several others. As a result a 12 h.p. experimental chassis was in progress in 1933 and 1934.

In May 1935 the first Brough Superior car proper was completed having a rating of 29 h.p., the engine being a Hudson straight eight in a Hudson chassis. This side-valve engine had cylinders 76×114 mm. 4,168 c.c., and there was a single-plate clutch connecting it to the three-speed (with one reverse) synchro-shift gearbox.

These were about the only major Hudson items retained and thus we find the new electrical equipment worked at 12 volts, two P170 Lucas headlamps were fitted as were a Serck radiator, hydraulic jacks and one central lubricating system for all points in the chassis. Messrs Atcherley of Birmingham constructed the handmade wooden bodywork, which was finished where necessary with genuine burr walnut. With a drop-head and a maximum speed of 90 m.p.h. with effortless silence it was priced at £695. His Grace the Duke of Richmond and Gordon took a personal interest in the car and its sales, which were in the able hands of Messrs Kevill-Davies and March Ltd. When ordered specially a supercharger by Messrs Shorrock Brothers could be fitted.

By June 1936 there appeared an additional model powered by a six-cylinder Hudson engine with cylinders $76 \cdot 2 \times 127$ mm. and of 21·6 h.p. For this a somewhat lighter body and chassis had been designed and a practically untouched photograph of a good example is shown in Fig. 71 against a typical English background. Brough Superior Cars Ltd called it a dual-purpose car because the head could be lowered in a few moments forming a flush line with the rest of the rear of the body.

Known also as the *Alpine Grand Sports* when supercharged, this special car would accelerate from zero to 60 m.p.h. in 9 seconds, to 80 m.p.h. in 16 seconds and to 100 m.p.h. in 35 seconds, its top speed

71 First Brough Superior car in a typical English setting

being at least 110 m.p.h. It was Mr Dixon's job to tune and pass out as correct each A.G.S. individually. A full specification will be found in Appendix H.

Offered in four forms, the Dual-Purpose Drophead unsupercharged was listed at £665, when supercharged £750, De Luxe Saloon unsupercharged £695, and the A.G.S. open four-seater £845.

In May 1938 there was offered to the public a new Brough Superior car using a Lincoln vee-twelve engine, wheels and brakes, the remainder of the vehicle being entirely Brough Superior in origin and

72 Offside view of the Vee 12 Brough Superior car

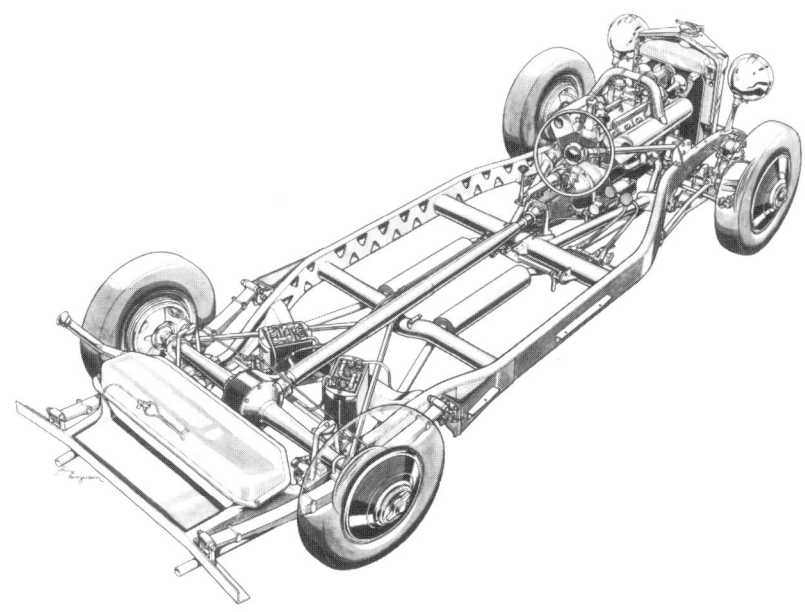

73   General arrangement of the car in Fig. 71

design. Rated at 37 h.p., this engine had cylinders 69·85 × 95·25 mm., 4,378 c.c., the two banks being arranged at 75°. With such a disposition of cylinders it was possible to include four mainshaft bearings, side-by-side connecting rods, all bearings being steel-shelled. All seatings of the side valves had tungsten alloy inserted seatings. Again a single dry-plate clutch is preferred between the engine and the three-speed box wherein the second and top gears were in synchromesh and the gears with helical teeth; the three ratios being 6·2, 3·8 and 1 to 1. Large air silencers were fitted to the dual downdraught carburettor and the cylinder heads were of aluminium alloy. An offside view is illustrated in Fig. 72 and I feel few will disagree if I venture to suggest that in spite of the 'double-ended' or streamlined cult so much in evidence today, this pre-war Brough Superior possessed the correct lines for a motor-car and therefore remains a machine of character.

An idea of the interesting features in the chassis may be gained from the line drawing in Fig. 73. Firstly, the maker did not lose sight of the fundamental point that for stability the centre of gravity

74 Further details of the Vee 12 car

must be as low as possible, and therefore we find the main framing is slightly below the centre-line of the transmission (it is under-slung at the rear end), rising a small amount at the front of necessity to clear the front axle. These main frames are no less than 6″ deep × $\frac{3}{16}$″ thick material and of box section. The widest part of the chassis is in the middle where its width equals the track of the wheels and where flexure might occur, and therefore we find the two tubular struts welded across as shown in the drawing. Naturally the rear has to be reduced in width a trifle to clear the wheels. In the front it is reduced somewhat more but on each side another tubular bracing connects the point of attachment of the rear ends of the front springs with the centre of the front cross-strut, thus thoroughly triangulating the front end. Advantage was taken of the centre and larger triangle to cradle the engine in it. Fig. 73 should be studied in conjunction with Fig. 74, which is a photograph showing still further details of the engine, chassis framing and front springing.

Meticulous care was bestowed upon the springs—all semi-elliptical —for each leaf 2½″ wide was tapered, ground and polished all over.

The front ones were placed perpendicularly beneath the chassis front sides and there was each side a bar connecting the front axle with the chassis side at a point close to the rear end of the spring, this bar being provided to take torsional stresses due to braking. At the rear the springs were underslung (as at the front) but were placed not parallel but wider at their front end than at their rear and all springs were damped by hydraulic shock-absorbers.

Some other features were twin Lucas P170 headlamps, twin Trippe fog lamps, automatic chassis lubrication, a spacious boot and a baffle under the bonnet to direct air and fumes from the engine under the vehicle. It is said a guardsman could hide in this spacious boot but this I have never checked!

Further main dimensions were a wheelbase of 10′ 8½″, front track standard railway gauge 4′ 8½″, rear 4′ 9½″, overall length 18′ 3″, overall width 5′ 11″, overall height 5′ 0″ and the tyres were 700×16 mm. Price of the chassis only was £850 but complete with saloon body £1,250. The first vee-twelve car was commenced on 10 December 1936 and completed in May 1938.

A little-known peculiarity originated on this car was the breaking of the bodywork radii at the rear to what is erroneously termed 'razor edge'. It was the first-ever use of this effect in any country. In view of the vogue it has become the maker tells me he wishes he had patented the idea!

A fitting conclusion to this chapter is to say the charming young lady at the wheel in Fig. 72 is none other than the then Miss Peggy Brough.

CHAPTER VIII

A Few Facts about the War Effort

Towards the end of Chapter Six I made passing reference to the war work undertaken at Vernon Road and referred to by George Brough in his wartime advertisements in the motor-cycling press.

At the tail end of 1938 and early in 1939 he had had prepared designs and a first-off sidecar machine having a drive to the sidecar wheel, the intention being to mount on it a machine-gun and lightly armour it. Also and alternatively by mounting a small pump it could be used as a fast mobile fire-fighting unit. As such it was offered to the British War Department and inspected by an official before the outbreak of war. The official turned it down, his reason being the Department's policy to use solo motor-cycles only, for despatch carrying. One can be pardoned for assuming this official had no knowledge or interest in motor-cycles and was quite unaware of the part played by similar outfits, made by the Bayerische Motoren Werke, in the German Army.

When this project failed George commenced making arrangements with the Ministry of Aircraft Production to undertake the manufacture of precision components, and such was his success that he was awarded his first contract on 10 September 1939—a week only after the declaration of war. Deliveries started in February 1940. Mainly the items were for Rolls Royce Merlin aero engines, and such work demanded a standard of precision and accuracy for which the manufacture of the Brough Superior in peacetime had adequately qualified the personnel. Once the works had been laid out and jigs and fixtures made it then became possible to take on and train an amount of female labour. In fact it became usual for the girls to work to $0.0001''$ on some jobs.

Some additions were made to the Vernon Road premises including a very efficient canteen, first-aid posts and facilities for recreation. Some land in close proximity to the works was used by employees for allotments whilst odds, ends and scraps from the canteen helped to maturity numbers of young pigs kept at one end of the yard, these pigs incidentally hailing from rural Lincolnshire, having been reared initially by a naval officer who owned a potent SS100. In addition, extra premises were acquired in Main Street, Bulwell (the next parish to Basford), and called No. 2 Works, and at the same time all the great quantity of valuable Brough Superior spares were satisfactorily housed.

After the disaster of Dunkirk much extra work in addition to actual contracts was taken on to help the output of vital parts in hand by several other famous firms.

It is only natural that absenteeism should become a problem, but by the autumn of 1942 there was introduced a rota system enabling not only the plant to be kept running 147 hours per week, but all employees to enjoy a fair share of leisure and recreation. As a result absenteeism was reduced to almost nothing. Sir Andrew Duncan called unexpectedly at midnight on one occasion in 1943 and after seeing for himself the high standard of work being turned out said to George Brough 'I congratulate you on having the happiest crowd of workers I have ever seen'. Here it will be opportune to record that the final finish on Rolls Royce crankshafts was obtained by lapping the pins and journals between two wooden slats hinged with a leather joint; the lapping compound being applied to a depression in the slats near their joint whilst the work was rotated between centres. The operator held the ends of the slats in his hands and drew the ends a little together. Thus were the mechanics of the ancient flail modified suitably for a later purpose. One is thus reminded of the motto of the Newcomen Society—*Actorem memores simul affectamus agenda*—Looking to the future one must always be mindful of the past.

Also during this period and with the approval of the department concerned experimental work was performed on two new prototype engines, further details of which will be found in Chapter Ten.

A fitting conclusion to this chapter is to record how during the war when stationed at Bulwell I was able to take parties of young officers over several works in the Nottingham area, and in particular on three occasions to Vernon Road. These visits proved most instructive I am pleased to say and we left with some increase in knowledge and happy memories of George's hospitality laid on for us in the canteen.

CHAPTER IX

Some Warriors at Ease

No story of the Brough Superior would be complete without some reference to the racing machines and the hardy men who managed and made them. We have already dealt with *Old Bill* and some of his successes fairly extensively in Chapter III where he falls more naturally into place. Here we will notice some of the machines and riders once very much in the eye of the motor-cycling public. I say 'some' because obviously for reasons of space it is not possible to cover more than a few of the machines which have gained glory, much as one would like to do so. A number of these glorious bicycles still exist—treasured—and like their owners, come out on special occasions as a change in their well-earned ease.

One of the first who comes to mind is Ronald W. Storey, the official work's tester and tuner from 1926 to 1946, now running a small business in Tollerton Green, Basford. He is also well known as Past President and now an active member of the B.S. Club. In fact, for the annual lunches of the Club in 1960 and 1961 it was he who undertook the rather thankless task of coping with most of the organising necessary for these occasions.

As a rider he possessed consummate skill combined with a considerate charming manner and pleasing temperament and all his riding was of the high-speed variety.

Storey presented himself before George in May 1926 armed with a letter of introduction from George Mills, Secretary of the Mansfield & District M.C.C., and was given a start in the works under Ike J. Webb. He did much work on the firm's sprint machine on which Arthur Greenwood made f.t.d. on the Sandall Beat alongside Doncaster Racecourse. Arthur's time was 18 sec. for the half-mile and it was the first time this track had been covered at 100 m.p.h. Storey was mechanic, van driver and as he told me 'the lot'! Towards the end of the year the maker decided he should take over the sprints and he (the maker), the sidecar events. Storey's first outing was at Blackpool in 1927 when George Patchett pipped him by only one-fifth of a second. After that he was rarely beaten and collected a fine

75   *Storey and the maker after winning the Doncaster Petrol St Leger*

bag of f.t.d.'s and course records. It was also in 1927 that he took to
sand racing and rode one of the three Brough Superiors at Pendine,
Tommy Spann riding one of the others. Unfortunately Ronald found
one notorious soft spot in the sands and after engine and frame had
bottomed in the sand, he and the bike parted company at only
15–20 m.p.h. Nevertheless he sustained blood poisoning from a
scratched leg which laid him low for fourteen weeks. However after a
fine recovery he rode at events up and down the country until the end
of 1927 when he personally and completely overhauled the works
sprinter with modifications tailored to suit him. The set of the bars,
saddle, footrests, knee grips and controls were all situated just so. It
paid off and throughout every meeting in 1928 it was firsts and f.t.d's,

and the Doncaster record went up to 101·7 m.p.h. With a standing start at Redcar Sands it was 101 m.p.h., on Lowestoft promenade he beat the fastest car, a Bugatti, passing it ten yards before the finish.

On a famous occasion at Brighton it was again fastest bicycle *v.* fastest car, then driven by Sir Malcolm Campbell. Storey was deemed to make a false start at the lights but a loose dog strayed on the course, fresh runs were allowed and as he put it to me, Campbell 'never saw the way I'd gone'!

Again at Pendine he was entered for the sprint and 100-mile races and was first in the former. Not so good in the long-distance event when the o.h.v. 1,000 shed both chains and part of the carburettor. There now followed a trip to Austria from which he returned as champion.

My own favourite Storey success is what I feel tempted to call his immortal effort at Saltburn Sands in 1928 when he returned the phenomenal figure of 18·2 seconds, equal to a course record of 122·9 m.p.h., a famous world record which remained unbroken until Bob Berry cracked it in 1947, nineteen years afterwards! Berry recorded an amazing lap in 17·8 seconds or 124·5 m.p.h. Even so, only 1·6 m.p.h. more!

The two smiling faces in Fig. 75 belong to R. W. Storey on the machine and George Brough standing by. Storey had just won the Doncaster Petrol St Leger in 1928 with the maker only ⅛ of a second slower.

It was in June 1928 that Storey was sent to Southport to see that a certain Pendine model was all ready for John H. (Jack) Carr to ride in the Southport 100.

Now Jack, way back in 1926, owned his own butchery business in Skipton, and at that time his mount was a single-cylinder machine of another make. One of his customers called one day on an SS80, the type with the 'lamp glass' silencers, and straightway Carr coveted his neighbour's goods. So much so that away went the single cylinder of another make plus an amount of ready cash in exchange. The silencers as Jack told me 'emitted a beautiful burbling note which was a joy to listen to'. In 1927 this was traded in for a new SS80, the owner taking the old one to the works. There he met several SS100's in brave array and succumbed. It was not long before he had part-exchanged the new SS80 for a new *Pendine* SS100 fitted with the 8/50 o.h.v. engine No. JTO/C 2792/T fed by a 'Mousetrap' 3-jet carburettor. Frame No. 950X and the complete ensemble ready for the course is seen on the trailer tailored to take it, in Fig. 76, a

76   *Jack Carr's famous* Pendine *racer*

compression ratio of 8·5 to 1 was used, the fuel being PNS2 alcohol obtained from the Hammersmith Distilleries. Wet-sump lubrication was employed, fed to the crankcase by a Pilgrim Duplex pump. Additional oil could be delivered to the cylinder walls by a hand pump operated by a handle-bar lever.

Now lubrication is most important, especially in racing, and so Jack's tactics were to have a mechanic stationed near where he changed gear at each half-lap during the longest sand races. This lad was armed with two handkerchiefs, one blue and one red. A blue meant a puff of exhaust smoke had been seen indicating adequate oiling. A red, however, indicated the opposite so that an extra charge was given as the next lap commenced. The Castle forks had been shortened slightly and the bicycle could be ridden hands-off in rough sand and it would always straighten out after a wobble. Slightly stronger springs and an extra plate were added to the clutch of the 3-speed heavyweight Sturmey-Archer gearbox.

So it is not surprising that success crowned Carr's efforts and in

May 1928 he won the 100-mile race at Flookborough Sands, the prizes being a fine gold cup and a free entry for the amateur T.T.

This performance quite impressed George, who invited Jack to send his machine to the works to be prepared for the Southport 100. A few modifications were carried out to the engine, a new larger tank fitted and Ronald Storey sent to see everything was correct. As the records show, Carr had the misfortune to drop the bicycle on the last corner letting Jimmy Simpson into first place. But he made amends winning the Southport 100 in 1931 and 1934 and the Southport 50 miles race and gold cup in 1933. Some of his fastest sprint times all at Southport were 114·5 m.p.h. in 1929, 108 in 1930, 101 in 1931 (with sidecar) and 110·7 in 1932. I hardly need add that Jack's great collection of gold and silverware fills a large and beautiful cabinet at his home, Haw Pike, Addingham.

In 1925 a certain Edwin Charles Ellis Baragwanath became acquainted with the house of the Brough Superior. An unusual surname perhaps, generally shortened to Barry, although another Baragwanath is a town in South Africa, but with which he had no connection, hailing as he did from Cambridge. In those days young men served a proper apprenticeship and Baragwanath served his seven years with the old Great Eastern Railway at Cambridge locomotive shops and afterwards gained still further experience with the Argyll Car Works in Glasgow and later helped in shipbuilding on the Thames. In this last-named job he was employed at the old Thames Ironworks Ltd., and it is most interesting to record that he worked on H.M.S. *Thunderer*, the last warship to be built on London River and launched on 1 February 1911. His first motor-cycle was a Minerva in 1908, and by 1912, the year he met Herbert le Vack, he was racing at Brooklands a 976 c.c. Winnitt-J.A.P., simultaneously carrying on his own automobile business in Camden Town. In a small acknowledgement like this it is impossible to enumerate all his feats as a solo rider as he was in his early days and later, as a sidecar exponent when, all told, he covered about 200 laps round the century mark at Brooklands including practice runs. Suffice it to say he held the Brooklands sidecar record three times, on a supercharged Brough Superior, at 101·69 in 1931, 103·11 in 1932 and finally 103·97 in 1933. This last record stood for some years until Noel Pope cracked it at 106·6 in 1938—using, incidentally, Baragwanath's outfit. Although no sidecar race on the track was won at a speed topping the century, Edwin Baragwanath came nearest with an average for three laps in 1933 of 99·22 m.p.h.

'Barry' commenced his Brough Superior association with an un-blown engine, but greatly modified to the extent of separate inlet elbows each mounting an A.M.A.C. TT 25 carburettor. For a short race the fuel used was RD1 but for long distances it was RD2, the compression ratio being 12·5 to 1. In sprints the compression ratio was increased to 14 to 1 and run on a mixture known only to the owner. For no accountable reason the *front* cylinder was found to overheat and this was combated by using a jet two sizes greater than the 70 used for the rear carburettor. Fuel consumption was usually little more than 10 m.p.g. Work on such a machine never ceases in the search for extra horse-power, and during further tuning the contours of the cams were altered to increase the overlap from 35° (the standard) to 60°. In addition the flywheels were lightened by careful machining to aid acceleration. Although no revolution counter was fitted Barry estimated that valve float took place at 6,500 r.p.m. and his method of gear changing was simply to snick the gear through without altering the full throttle, when float took place. In October 1927 he pushed up records for the world's sidecar for the kilometre and mile standing start to 74·96 and 80·5 respectively. In 1929 up he put them again to 75·74 and 83·32, and that on a foggy day when he reckoned his maximum was around 106 m.p.h.! In 1928 he won the Brooklands 200 miles sidecar race at nearly 74 and in 1930 he lapped at 99 m.p.h. Neither was Barry unknown elsewhere, for he put up the fastest time of the day at Southport, Brighton, Essingdon, Southend, Lewes and Lowestoft. It is very curious but a fact that at Lowestoft his standing start one-way kilometre speed was then faster than the current world's sidecar record!

Small wonder then that near the end of 1930 the potent J.A.P. had had enough and finally disintegrated. So a new 8/50 was ordered from Tottenham and Barry incorporated with it a Powerplus supercharger Type B eccentrically mounted between aluminium plates as seen in Fig. 77. The carburettor was a special car-type Amal requiring two $\frac{5}{16}$"-bore pipes to feed the three jets, the consumption proving to be a mere 4 m.p.g. At first the front cylinder again overheated to such an extent that one lap of Brooklands at full bore was enough to cause serious trouble. My own opinion is that this was due to the super-charger supplying boost at 15 p.s.i. during the long time the crank-shaft turned 410° (see Fig. 89), thus giving a very rich charge. In the case of the rear cylinder the boost was supplied during the short time the crankshaft turned 310°. Barry overcame this defect by reducing the peak lift of the front inlet cam by $\frac{1}{16}$" and reducing the compression

77 E. C. E. Baragwanath's supercharged machine after a Brooklands lap at 103·97 m.p.h.

ratio of the front cylinder from 7 to 6·8 to 1. The later photograph in Fig. 78 incidentally shows this famous record-breaker restored to its original state as when raced by Baragwanath and is now in the ownership of C. E. Allen, Esq., of the Brough Superior Club. With this new outfit Barry took the records noted in an earlier paragraph. Additionally he covered a half-mile at no less than 116·88 m.p.h. along the Railway Straight between the Members' and Byfleet Bankings. This be it remembered was more than thirty years ago! But a man cannot race for ever and in 1933 (his fiftieth year) he bowed gracefully to the inevitable—and retired. I make no apology for reproducing the well-known picture in Fig. 77, showing as it does Barry and his passenger Edward Sidcup after winning the 3-lap sidecar race at 99·22 m.p.h. in 1933, the fastest lap being covered at 103·97 m.p.h. It is one of the 'great' pictures in the history of motorcycling.

It is here I must close this brief narrative of Edwin Baragwanath. He was every ready with helpful advice and was a fountain of knowledge, and on a pinnacle by himself when it came to craftsmanship in engine building and fitting. He possessed too a greater than ordinary share of courage. For instance, to test a magneto he just held the end of the lead and spun the instrument. His death although not altogether unexpected, on 8 September 1961, was a great loss to all

78   Baragwanath's famous racer in its final and present form

big twin enthusiasts, and it is sad to realise that never again shall we see that immaculate starched wing collar protruding from overalls or jacket. It is a comfort to think the Baragwanath Cup, donated by his sister (Mrs V. D. Spencer) and competed for every year at the annual rally of the Brough Superior Club, will keep his name alive.

Major Noel Baddow Pope needs little introduction I feel, having been acquainted with Brooklands as early as March 1933, the year Barry retired. A man of many parts, Pope was at home as mechanic, actor (like his late father), writer, painter, property surveyor, army officer, record-breaker and so on, indeed a veritable Pooh-Bah in real life. In the month before-mentioned he covered the flying kilo-metre at 70·34 m.p.h. on a 350 c.c. Zenith powered by the ubiquitous Tottenham-made engine. Then followed great happiness with a one-litre British Anzani which enabled him to win a Gold Star with a lap of 105·7 m.p.h. Later came the chance to acquire Barry's super-charged machine. He acquired it, then returned fastest time of the day at Gatwick (11·53 secs., 78 m.p.h. for standing quarter-mile), and Brighton speed trials. During the coming winter he put his engineer-ing training from London University to excellent use and on the

79 *Details of Noel B. Pope's engine for the post-war record*

80 *The complete machine housing the supercharged engine seen in Fig. 79*

Wednesday afternoon following T.T. week in 1935 (his junior Velocette caught fire and he cancelled his senior entry to return home), he lapped Brooklands at 120·59 thus qualifying for a Double Gold Star, one of two such awards ever to be struck.

Raced with a sidecar in 1937 he literally drove the big outfit (the first time he had had the sidecar attached), round to win his sidecar Gold Star at 103·5 m.p.h. Shortly afterwards he returned 106·6 which, Brooklands being no more alas, makes his sidecar record a permanent holding. There followed on 6 July 1935, during a three-lap handicap, a lap at 120·59. But the record was short-lived because Eric Fernihough, on a competing Brough Superior, returned an answering lap at 123·58 on the 27th of the same month. With the dogs of war a bit vociferous in Europe Pope made haste to regain the outer lap record and did so, for on 4 July 1939 he put up the classic Brooklands achievement of all time—a lap at 124·51 m.p.h. Thus for evermore will the solo and sidecar lap records stand to Pope and the Brough Superior.

Two little points arise worth comment concerning the solo record. The time taken was 80 seconds. Now the lap distances round that famous concrete saucer vary somewhat. For instance, at the inner edge the distance is 2·7054 miles, at the outer edge 2·8284 miles and at the 90-feet line, i.e. 10 feet from the outer edge, it is 2·8161 miles. The corresponding speeds for a lap in 80 seconds are 121·74, 127·28 and 126·72 m.p.h. respectively. As Noel was for most of the lap between the 90-feet line and the outer edge his actual speed was near enough 127 m.p.h.

After the span of the war years Pope had a crack at the world's solo record of 174 m.p.h. made on 28 November 1937 by Ernst Henne at Frankfurt-am-Main, Germany. This time he was one of a team comprising himself, A. E. T. Comerford and George Brough. They sailed on 13 August 1949 to Salt Lake City with the prepared machine sent on ahead. Seen in Fig. 79 the supercharged engine has forward-facing exhaust ports, twin magnetos, or very much the same as it was when it gained the two Brooklands all-time records. However, the machine was overhauled at Nottingham and the engine at Tottenham. A new blower by the Wade Engineering Co. of Gatwick was mounted in the same position forward of the front engine plates, as the Powerplus people could not supply spares. This is shown more clearly in a view of the complete machine seen in Fig. 80 but without the streamline shell. Most of the bicycle parts were unaltered although the engine was improved with a new crankcase and new barrels, the

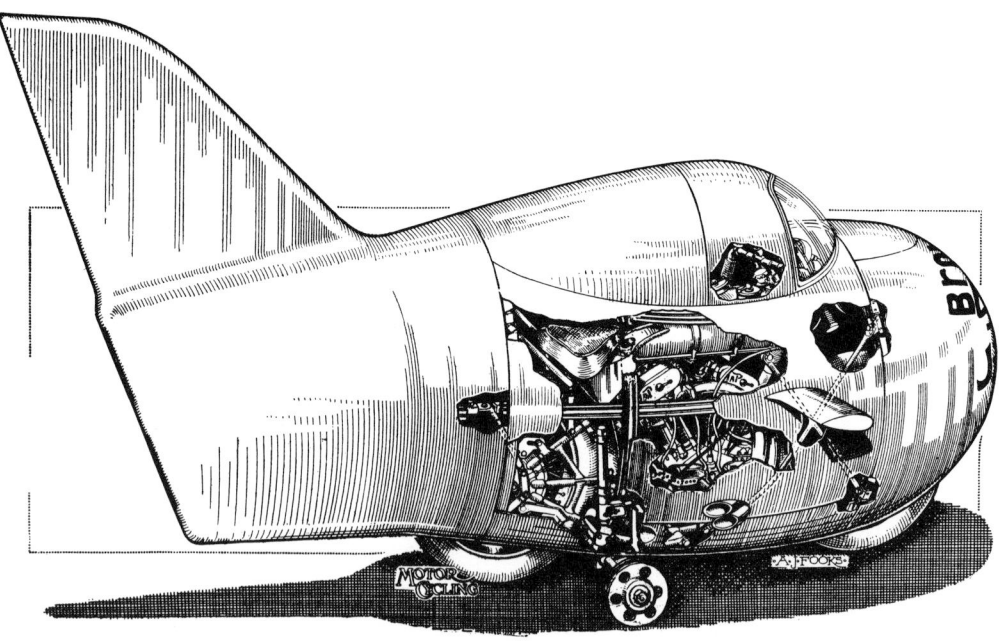

81 Pope's design of streamlining in 1949

remainder being as used before the war. Much has been written and published and which is available to the interested enthusiast so only a short résumé of the streamlining can be given here. Pope did much personal pioneer work on the shape of a suitable shell, later checked at the aerodynamics laboratory of Blackburn & General Aircraft Ltd, and the result of all this hard work is to be seen in Fig. 81. Wind-tunnel tests showed that the top rear stabilising fin was essential, as without it the bicycle could get out of hand even in a slight sidewind, and the result could be disastrous if this state coincided with both wheels airborne at the same moment. Briefly, by using the shell the drag coefficient was calculated to be 0·00024 whereas for a T.T. machine in usual racing trim this figure would average 0·00078—hence the value of streamlining at very high speeds. Unfortunately, after all these monumental efforts to regain the coveted 'World's Fastest' for England, Pope and the machine parted company at 150 or so on the Bonneville Salt Lake of Utah and after that the party returned home and the Brough did little more serious racing. It is given to few men to crash a solo at this velocity and walk away!

Eric Fernihough is a name known, not only to Brough Superior enthusiasts, but to countless motor-cyclists the world over, so it is difficult to add to all that which is common knowledge. Eric began racing as early as 1923, his speciality in those days being 175 c.c. machines. In fact, he broke the Brooklands lap record for this class at 86·92 m.p.h. Altogether, all his wins and records totalling eighty or more have been achieved with J.A.P. engines. Considering in particular his big twins, we find he first used them unsupercharged, attaining on Brooklands saucer 136 and later 141 m.p.h. After fitting a supercharger he was able to cover the second quarter mile on the track at 150 m.p.h. when the bicycle was found to be still accelerating. In 1937 on 19 April he tackled the world's record and returned 169·786 m.p.h. to secure it once again for his country. In addition he broke the flying mile at 168·5. Both sidecar records fell to him that April day with 137 for the kilometre and 135 for the flying mile respectively. In one direction he achieved 175 m.p.h. over the kilometre but on the return run the crankshaft sprocket key sheared, an unheard-of trouble. He had designed a detachable streamlined shell for this attempt, similar to Pope's configuration although without the elevated tail fin, but found he could touch 175 without it. In regaining the above record he used only the front fork cowling or helmet and the egg-ended tailpiece.

During the autumn and winter of 1937–8, new streamlining was

82   Fernihough at speed at the Crystal Palace

made and fitted to the same machine, those parts enshrouding the engine and rear meeting sufficiently short of each other to form a space for the rider's legs, the fork cowling or helmet being retained. The engine, virtually a double single, had the Zoller supercharger chain-driven in front of the crankcase with a pressure gauge on the induction pipe. During a try-out at Brooklands on 13 March 1938 he covered the measured kilometre along the Railway Straight at no less than 143·39 m.p.h. A view of Eric at speed on this streamlined machine at the Crystal Palace in 1937 is included in Fig. 82.

But beating Ernst Henne by less than one mile per hour was not enough for Fernihough and the Brough and so we find him and his staunch mechanic R. C. Rowland, loading their Ford station wagon for Gyon once again when on 23 April 1938 at 3·15 a.m. they unloaded the record-breaker on that straight Hungarian main road. Well after sunrise Rowland tested the wind's force by seeing its effect on a blanket after which Fernihough set off round the approach bend for the timed straight. Rowland's evidence that by the sound of it the big J.A.P. was clocking at least 180 m.p.h. cannot be denied, and it was half-way along that the gust caught him and the front end lifted off the ground—as appalling luck would have it on that short portion of the straight bordered by a kerb. The front wheel descending hit the kerb, putting the machine in line with one of only three small tree stumps at that part. Had the stump not been there, Eric might have kept control. As it was he never regained consciousness.

A tall man but far stronger than his looks suggested, Fernihough possessed a sense of dry humour, not always immediately apparent which, combined with some innocent superstitions, serve as an index to his character. To race on the thirteenth of the month was not lucky, black cats were, and will account for this emblem seen on the front cowling during that memorable attempt on the world's record. With both a scientific and a logical mind, after graduating at Cambridge Fernihough established a tuning business beside the Brooklands track. It was here that all his tuning and preparations were made to the two machines which featured at events at home and at Gyon. It is a sad but by no means unfamiliar fact that England seldom encourages its heroes, and so we are not surprised to find no official backing was ever afforded Fernihough in his quest to regain the world's fastest for his country; neither from the Government in the form of closure of an appropriate road, nor from the motor-cycle industry and its allied trades. For example, he found it was impossible to hire a dynamometer at a reasonable fee and he could not get the use of a wind tunnel to check his empirical streamline enclosures. Had he had this benefit, afforded Noel Pope later, it is conceivable he would be with us today. When he did regain the record in 1937 some of the daily newspapers did just mention it and how it must have revolted them. Only one individual emerges from this sorry tale with great credit, George Brough. For it was he who with his characteristic generosity made it 'easy' for Eric Fernihough to acquire his two record-breakers.

There the matter of attempts to regain the world's fastest for this country might have rested, but the spirit of the big vee twin dies hard. Contemporaneously with the exploits of Pope and Fernihough before the Second World War, a certain Robert Berry wrote in 1936 to Haydn Road, about any fast bicycle there might be for disposal. Now Bob Berry hailed from Skipton and so did Jack Carr, and it might have been more than mere coincidence that Berry's enquiry arrived when Carr's racing machine (Jack had just given up racing), was first available for a likely aspirant to high speed. Being of part Yorkshire descent myself I like to think so.

This fine old 8/50 J.A.P. did very well during its new lease of life, and enabled its new owner to gather many firsts at sand-race meetings up and down the country. In 1938, as speeds had been increasing gaily, Bob purchased one of the new 8/75 engines from Tottenham. It had four float chambers in a row—'looks like a row of pint pots on a pub shelf' as Freddie Dixon once remarked—and Berry reached 126 m.p.h. on it along the straights at Southport. Even so this was still not fast enough, so one of the 'two of everything' 8/80 J.A.P. engines based on Stanley M. Greening's design was acquired in 1939. This engine it may be remembered had been evolved partly for the F. W. D. Skirrow dirt track cars and was used also in the 1,000 c.c. Cooper cars, one of which driven by Stirling Moss reached over 150 m.p.h. Berry's own experience was that with the new engine in the Brough, it proved to be faster in second than the previous engine had been in top gear. Its first appearance at Southport won for him the mile sprint although he stayed in second gear for the entire field in eight laps. Unfortunately on the tenth lap seawater shorted the front plug and when power cut in again on full throttle the instantaneous loading broke the crankpin. However, Tottenham came to the rescue with a new engine. All was well again because at Hartlepool Speed Trials on the Saturday before war broke out Berry and the new engine made the fastest time of the day.

After the war years when peace had broken out the 8/80 won the

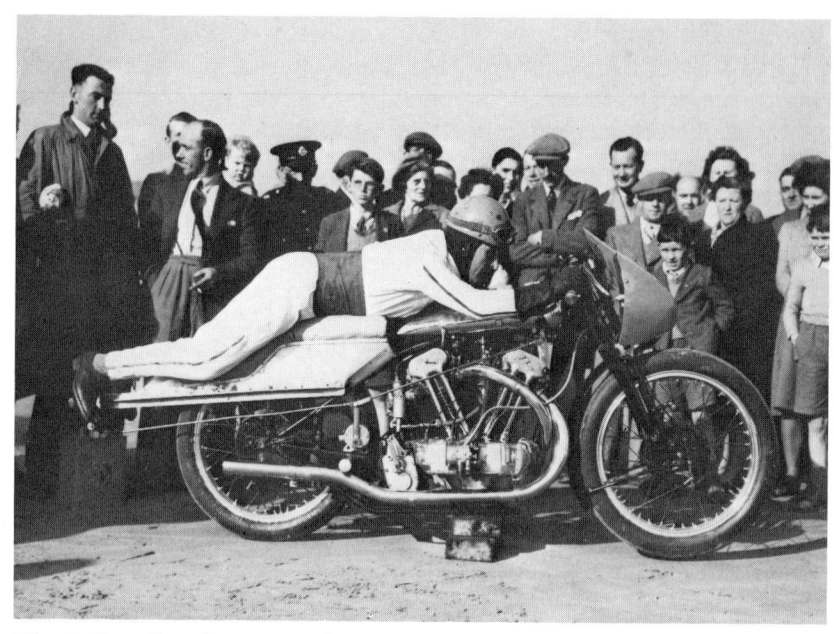

83 *Robert Berry's prone riding position*
84 *Two-of-everything 8/80 J.A.P. engine used by Berry*

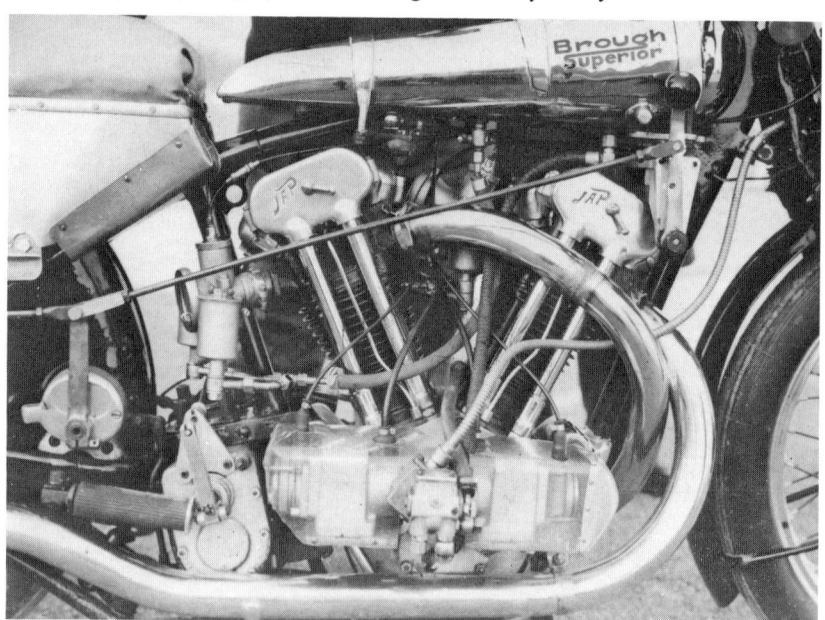

mile sprint at Pendine by half a mile, in second gear only again, leaving the 8/75 machine to win the 10- and 25-mile races. When Berry was leading in the 50-mile race the Burman gearbox split clean in two, the lower half complete with layshaft dropping off. Then followed the fastest time of the day at Hartlepool, Queensferry and Brighton and successes at many meetings in 1946, 1947 and 1948.

One occasion stands out above all others, viz. the Yorkshire Sand Race Meeting at Redcar on 12 July 1947, which venue had taken the place of the Saltburn site a few miles away. After the straight mile events came the attempts on the local flying kilometre sand record put up to 122·9 by Ronald Storey way back in 1928. Berry tackled it against a sharp head wind and returned 114·12. But towards the end of the meeting the stewards wisely decided another run was justified. By then, some three hours later, the vagaries of the English climate had not only reduced the wind but veered it round 180°. This time with everything favourable the unblown Brough did it in 17·8 seconds —124·5 m.p.h. But as I mentioned before only 1·6 m.p.h. faster. If this provides some idea of Storey's achievement nineteen years previously, it also underlines Berry's prowess in 1947. Both in my opinion were wins in a class by themselves. These occasions have not been without some hectic moments, as for example, when diving between the columns beneath Saltburn Pier at not much under 100 m.p.h.!

For a long time Berry has been of the opinion that had Eric Fernihough's streamlining been aerodynamically correct and with the power of the blown J.A.P. at his disposal, Eric could have exceeded 250 m.p.h. So during the off-season of 1948–9 Bob prepared the big machine for timed runs at Pendine, the engine being returned to Tottenham for a general check-up. The amazing thing was that although he had raced the Brough for three years he had never had it all-out in top gear. For example, it reached 128 at Brighton in second gear using the three-speed box and crossed the finishing line at 140 m.p.h. in top after a missed change. Later at Pendine in April 1949 on a beach as hard as iron he reached 162 m.p.h. To reduce wind resistance Berry had developed and adopted the fully prone riding position as will be seen from Fig. 83. Perfect weather conditions did not re-appear at Pendine until 1960 and on that occasion the machine and rider reached 186 m.p.h. in third gear—recorded by a Spitfire-type airspeed indicator, renowned for its accuracy. But conditions rapidly deteriorated on the beach, the next-best being 140, owing to off-sea winds and broken-up sand. Further details of the 'two of everything' engine are shown in Fig. 84 where the twin magnetos are enclosed in cellophane to exclude sand and water. Note too the ingenious gear-change mechanism, which can be operated either by the right hand or right toe when the rider is in the prone position, the complete layout being apparent from the full offside view in Fig. 83. Other interesting points about the engine were hairpin valve springs, Alfin barrels with large fins, iron heads, forged pistons and dry-sump lubrication. The large fins kept the pistons remarkably cool whilst the iron heads heated up very quickly aiding the vaporisation of alcohol fuel and so cut down the warming-up period—a not unimportant point when the weather was inclined to be changeable. But conditions remained unfavourable for attempting world's records and in September Berry landed in Belgium to participate in the speed and records week on the Jabbeke Motorway. Although I have no use for the idiot who praises in enthusiastic tone all centuries but this and every country but his own, I must admit they organise races better in Belgium, for here the wide main road was closed from the Monday to the Friday. Berry started in the dawn mists on the Wednesday having geared the big twin for 180 m.p.h. at 7,000 r.p.m. in top and for 157 in second at 7,400. The big engine started at once and after fitting hotter plugs he opened up to 100 in bottom, changing and taking the engine up to 7,600 in second (over 155 m.p.h.), when there was a bang from the transmission. The layshaft had broken. A hurried rush to Ostend, telephone to Vernon Road and Donald Webb set off with three new layshafts to London Airport which were flown to Brussels. After working all night the machine was ready again but the weather was gales, heavy rain and thunderstorms. By accurate observation Bob had noticed that the first half-hour after dawn and the last half-hour of daylight are usually periods of comparative calm, and it was during the evening calm that he made another attempt. With a 10 m.p.h. diagonal headwind he found the bicycle too high-geared, only 5,200 in top (151 m.p.h.). Now there are two bridges over the road on the measured mile and naturally the wind is suddenly cut off and restored when passing beneath. The effect of this at 150 or more was to force rider and machine on to the grass for 300 yards! However courage is a marvellous thing, Berry kept the throttle open, finished the timed length and coasted to rest two miles further on where he turned round and waited for the green Verey light to herald the timing gear set for the return run. This time he kept in second gear at 7,600 r.p.m. which was faster than 5,200 in top and screamed the engine right through the timed stretch—it being now almost dark! The south–north run was done at 152·8, the north–south

85 *Berry's form of streamlining for the prone riding position*

run at 159 giving an average of 155·9—the fastest in Belgium. As Goldie Gardner had broken his record on his M.G. earlier in the week the Saturday night party left nothing to be desired.

During the winter of 1959–60 Berry stripped and rebuilt the big machine completely, this time fitting his own design of streamlining seen in the photograph reproduced in Fig. 85. By July 1961 it was ready but such was the atrocious weather that it was the third Sunday in August before an attempt could be made. As the sun broke through, out came machine and man, and clad only in pullover and slacks Bob decided to make a slow run along the beach, just to see how things were. The engine fired at once and he proceeded in bottom gear to 80 changing into second at 90 or so and tucking himself into the shell glanced at the revolution counter: 140 m.p.h.! As he put it to me 'I hadn't even put on my crash hat'. During the return run the wind increased to 30 m.p.h. when the machine became almost unmanageable. By 4.30 the wind had dropped to 5 m.p.h. and what proved to be the last attempt was made. After a change to second at 90 the acceleration was fantastic to 150 when with a quick dab by foot it was in top. He held 160 for a quarter of a mile and then opened to full bore—too quickly, for wheelspin set in and the rear wheel slid out of line when, with the enormous air pressure the machine was forced over at 167 m.p.h. and both hit the sand. Bob rolled himself into a ball, felt his collarbone snap as he hit the sand and rolled 70 yards or more, the bicycle covering about half a mile.

During the weeks he spent in Carmarthen Hospital Berry came to one conclusion, viz. that another record-breaker would have to be

111

86 *Harold Karslake's* Karbro Express

conceived on new and original lines entirely. The procedure must be reversed, i.e. the machine must be put in the shell designed previously, not the shell ranged round the machine. Then he would install the engine and himself inside it—precisely as was done later by Craig Breedlove and William Johnson in 1963. It meant that an entirely new type of low-slung frame and steering head assembly would have to be made for the job. Bob Berry deceased November 1970 in Carmarthen Hospital.

So for the time being the gallant Brough with over 500 'firsts' in its long life (1928–50) has gone into retirement. There have been so many great Broughs but this enabled its owner to become Britain's fastest motor-cyclist. I wonder if it is the greatest of them all?

One great individual who certainly qualifies for mention here is the late Harold Karslake, known, as I pointed out earlier on, as 'Oily'. His first association with the family of Brough was in 1910 in the London–Edinburgh trial with George Brough 'Junr', as he was then styled, coming first. Harold Karslake managed second. Again in 1911 George was first and Karslake second. In those days the trial was run there and back. In 1912 history repeated itself—George first again with Harold second riding a Rover. After service in the R.F.C., later R.A.F., Karslake took the job of manager to William Brough in the original old works in Vernon Road. In 1920 he even helped to produce his first '90 Bore' Brough Superior in George's then small works, although he really paid for it! He entered it in the Land's End trial next year winning a Gold—the first incidentally to be awarded to a Brough Superior rider in this national classic. After this he aided George in various capacities and as we have noticed, was mainly responsible for the prop stand, pannier bags, the 'set' of the later handlebars and other items conducive to luxury riding. In 1928 he again indulged in machine building, on this occasion using a Brough frame and tank housing a special '90 Bore' J.A.P. engine with a stroke extended to 118 mm. providing 1,497 c.c., making it the machine with probably the biggest-capacity engine regularly ridden on the road. Appropriately enough he christened it the *Karbro Express*, and it is to be seen in Fig. 86 with its owner-builder at the start of the 1928 London–Edinburgh run. Its compression ratio incidentally was $4\frac{1}{2}$ to 1 and at 80 m.p.h. it was comparatively inaudible. The history of motor-cycling is most indebted to Harold Karslake! He was, too, a founder member of the A.P.M.C., its librarian up to the time of his death at the age of eighty-two in 1962, vice-president of the Vintage Motor Cycle Club and life member of the M.C.C. At the age of seventy-four, an age when most car drivers are physically and mentally incapable of riding even a pushbike, Karslake competed in and finished the Edinburgh Commemorative Run in 1954 on an LE Velocette, an event remembered for the severity of its weather.

In addition he spent much time on testing the three-cylinder radial engines to be mentioned briefly in the next chapter, and gave freely his advice on certain aspects of the design of the engine for the *Dream*:

It was my privilege to know Harold for many years, and his wife from beyond the Tweed, and to enjoy their kindness and hospitality. Ally to this enjoyment his kindly disposition, his encyclopaedic knowledge of mathematics, of physics and of engineering and one has a personality rarely to be met with and certainly never to be forgotten by the writer.

All warriors, whether at ease or not, rely on the armourer for their weapons, and I think this is the proper place to remember some of the 'lads' behind the scenes, right-hand men to the rider-designer-manufacturer and with whom all the riders and owners who knew the works must have been on friendly terms. Such as Stanley Whysall of the toolroom. He started with George's father in 1918, who told him 'If a job is worth doing it is worth doing well, and two wrongs don't make a right', and it was this thorough grounding in the fundamentals and W. E. Brough's insistence there was no such thing as 'can't' which helped Stanley to achieve the great degree of accuracy needed in I.C. engine work. As I mentioned much earlier on, Brough senior was often ahead of his time, and many operations in casting, forging and heat treatment were undertaken at Vernon Road at a period when such work was usually attempted by specialist firms in Sheffield. Stanley Whysall worked on tools and jigs for all the Model G engines and a $3\frac{1}{2}$ h.p. flat twin was used in a lawn mower made at that time for William Brough's personal use. As he put it to me 'I was the only youth who could cut grass at 20 m.p.h.'! Today, in spite of occasional illness, Stanley is still actively engaged on work requiring extreme accuracy.

Contemporary with Whysall was Ike Webb, now Life President of the Brough Superior Club. Everyone met and got to know Ike sooner or later, and who in later years was works manager until he moved to take up a directorship with Messrs Blacknell Sidecars Ltd. Ike started with George in the Stockhill Lodge days and so grew up, as it were, with the Brough Superior. Not minding if he were sometimes late home, he put in a great amount of time on rush jobs to oblige customers, and so became perhaps a little better known than others working in deeper recesses in the works. During the First World War Ike saw service in the Grenadier Guards and the Royal Marine Artillery, and was attached to some of the heaviest ordnance then in use. For his services rendered at the works on wartime contracts from 1939 to 1945, Ike received a B.E.M. in 1946. Needless to say he has a grand store of information about the Brough Superior which three-and-seventy years has not dimmed in the least. On one occasion he was speechless. The late Herbert Le Vack collected the work's scrapper preparatory to an attempt on the world's fastest. It had been meticulously prepared and upon departing Le Vack said he would strip the whole machine before the meeting, such was his thoroughness. Thoughtfully he added, 'You don't mind George, do you'? I am told Ike's face was worth seeing. So was George's!

Like Ike Webb, Donald (Donnie) Webb, his younger brother spent all his life with the family of Brough, first with William and latterly with George. He specialised in engine building and after the Second World War took charge of the 'hut' along one side of the yard where all post-war rebuilding and repairs were carried out. Many are the times I have tarried in the hut to see what bicycles were in for repairs and for despatch. In addition one learnt much. Always friendly, his premature death in 1960 was a great shock and loss to many older Brough riders. Like Baragwanath he is not forgotten, for his daughter Diana has presented a cup to the Brough Superior Club for annual competition.

One of the most important men in any works is the storekeeper. Not only must he run the stores but a really good keeper can render enormous help to users of the product by advice, identification of parts, and so on. So it is with Leslie Fearn the present keeper, who always attends Club events and gives freely his advice and arranges for spares to be sent and even made, if out of stock. Not content with this he has more than once helped with arrangements for these functions and played no small part in aiding Ronald Storey to organise the luncheon held in Wollaton Park in 1960.

Older owners may remember Clement Cripwell who managed the counting house as one of his major rôles. At one period, it is said, he could tell most owner's names if given the registration numbers of their machines! He is still actively engaged in business in Nottingham.

Then there was William Smith, Cripwell's right-hand man at one time, who owned an early SS80 with narrow tank. He later left to enter the hotel business and at one time was mine host of the hotel in Clumber Park.

A leading mechanic was Ted Lester, with whom a few customers may have become acquainted when discussing repairs. Most of the cleaning and packing was performed after 1925 by the inimitable Jack Browning whom George reminded me 'was a character on his own'. More of a handyman than a mechanic, Jack would do anything for anybody to help keep the flag he loved best flying high—the B.S. flag.

Messrs Smith, the two Webbs and Browning we have already met forming the background to Fig. 26. The nickel and chromium plating was in the care of George Stevenson who spent seventy-three of the eighty-six years of his life with the firm, helped by Albert the polisher; with F. Stevenson another tuner, rider and tester, not omitting Eric Peacock also an engine builder. Let us not forget many of the staff, additional to those mentioned above who have been with George from fifteen to thirty years. Stanley Whysall's total is forty-five years in fact, as he commenced with W. E. Brough.

Lastly, we will conclude with Douglas Wesson who, like many of the foregoing, worked with George's father initially. When George took over the Basford Works in 1937, Douglas became his private secretary, a post he still holds. Here again many owners have been indebted to his knowledge and help.

Seldom do Brough Superior riders meet together but that some anecdote or other is brought to mind, and the experience related. In fact an amusing, instructive and entertaining book could be written devoted entirely to Brough tales. Here is what happened to an old Brough enthusiast, Roger North, Esq., of Rougham Hall, Norfolk, when at Cambridge. His mount was one of the famous '90 Bores' and on one occasion after a bout of high speed the front cylinder head burst from the top of the barrel. Nothing daunted and with no permission to be out very late, North cut a piece of sapling with which he plugged the end of the inlet pipe usually reserved for the front head and got back on the rear cylinder. Being busy with lectures he had to use it thus for nearly a week until a new barrel could be fitted. His only slight criticism to me was 'instead of usually touching eighty, I was restricted to a maximum of fifty'!

Then there was the occasion of Frederick Dixon at Doncaster Speed Trials. George Brough, Storey, Dixon and others had all had a very happy and successful afternoon's racing, but on returning to the car and trailer parked alongside the boundary fence, Dixon caught a pickpocket trying to 'lift' something off the trailer. Now Freddie was exceedingly strong for his height and without word-wasting he seized the wretched wrongdoer, lifted him chest-high with both hands and literally shot him over the fence to become a body falling freely under the force of gravity. The body did not re-appear!

But there must be a curtailment of tales and so I must finish with the young gentleman, son of a gentleman, who came to Haydn Road (before it was tarred and made up), to take delivery of a new SS100. As this youth was experienced only in the matter of 350 c.c. or so, Ike Webb thought it advisable to offer a few words of advice and started to explain the position of the controls, the general character-istics and the great surge of power available, but the young customer seemed to know all. The big engine was started up and the group at the top of the ramp—George, Ike and Donald Webb and Smith, watched the newcomer accelerate down the slope, across the earth-bound road and raze several yards of the fencing on the opposite side finishing up in the rough terrain! It altered considerably the con-figuration of the Castle forks. The group just looked at each other, for occasionally silence speaks stronger than sound, and muteness becomes more eloquent than eloquence!

So far we have dealt with just a few of the great names in racing and touring leaving one character and Brough Superior enthusiast who cannot be classified at all. Of many famous non-racing owners and riders, perhaps the most illustrious was the late Colonel T. E. Lawrence. To historians of the standard type he appears in some respects to be somewhat of a mystery. Whilst I make no pretence to assess his character—it would be a brave man indeed who did so—I venture to suggest insight into his complex nature may be found in his great love of motor-cycling. One cannot imagine those, so far, who have written on Lawrence being in any way sympathetic to motor-cycles. In fact, one gathers the opinion that in their ignorance they regard all single-track vehicles and their associated lack of snob value with abhorrence. For example, one foreign writer in a recent publication on Lawrence referred to him in one place and 'a motor-cycle'! In his own writings Lawrence discloses a liking for his own company, a liking we all know easily fostered by ownership of a fast solo. Here in his own words I think is the key to much that is not clear about him:

It's usually my satisfaction to purr along gently about 60 m.p.h. drinking in the air and the general view. I lose detail even at such moderate speeds but gain comprehension. When I open out a little more, as for instance across Salisbury Plain at 80 or so, I feel the earth moulding herself under me. It is *me* piling up this hill, hollowing this valley, stretching out this level place. Almost the earth comes alive, heaving and tossing on each side like a sea. It is the reward of speed. I could write you pages on the lustfulness of moving swiftly.

Clearly the feeling of a poet and mystic.

Now this makes it very awkward for the said standard authors when writing on Lawrence; how much easier it would be for them had he preferred a fast motor-car, or even a yacht. A similar situation comes to mind involving Sir Arthur Sullivan. How annoying of him to compose work after work so delectable to his average fellow men when, as the snob critics would have us believe, he should have written only oratorios and very grand opera! But unfortunately for them and fortunately for us Lawrence preferred a big solo and a Brough Superior at that—the perfect medium enabling him to project his complex personality as it suited him. For example he left Haydn Road one Tuesday at 4.30 p.m. and arrived back at 4.50 a.m. the following Friday with his rear tyre incredibly worn. An understanding of what this entails—the intensity of motive and its fulfilment—is a key to many of his exploits on foreign soil and to his mental behaviour. This intensity of motive had often been paralleled previously, as for example, when with the dictatorship over the Arabs within his reach after his Palestine campaign, he set up a government for them and after three days returned home. One of those rare occasions in world history where power did not corrupt.

Altogether Lawrence had seven Brough Superiors between the years 1922 and 1935 comprising one SS80 and six SS100's. There has been too much nonsense written about Lawrence and his machines and even in 1963 one writer tried to perpetuate the old legend that he was responsible for machine design, acted as tester and generally wheedled machines out of the manufacturer. The facts are, as George points out, that Lawrence was never a works tester (we must remember Ronald Storey), that he never produced an engineering design (we must remember Harold Karslake), and that list prices were paid for his bicycles. I think some confusion may have arisen because our subject did keep an accurate and detailed diary of his motorcycling and his journeys, noting any defect which might develop and its repair, fuel and oil consumption, tyre wear and so on. This was accompanied by the applicable mileage and he called them History Sheets. It was only natural he would acquaint the maker with some of these findings, and this may have given rise to the statements to which I have referred. In eleven years Colonel Lawrence covered 299,000 miles or over 27,000 miles a year.

Before going abroad once he sent the following letter to George:

Yesterday I completed 100,000 miles since 1922 on five successive Brough Superiors, and I am going abroad very soon, so that I think I must make an end, and I thank you for the road pleasure I have got out of them. In 1922, I found George I (your old Mark I) the best thing I'd ridden, but George V (the 1926 SS100) is incomparably better. In 1925 and 1926 (George IV and V), I have not had an involuntary stop, and so have not been able to test your spares service, on which I drew so heavily in 1922 and 1923. Your present machines are as reliable and fast as Express Trains, and the greatest fun in the world to drive—and I say this after twenty years' experience of cycles and cars.

They are expensive to buy, but light in upkeep (50–65 m.p.g. of petrol, 4,000 m.p.g. of oil, 5,000–6,000 miles per outer cover, in my case), and in the four years I have only made one Insurance claim (for less than £5), which is a testimony to the safety of your controls and designs. The SS100 holds the road extraordinarily. It's my great game on a really pot-holed road to open up to 70 m.p.h. or so, and feel the machine gallop; and though only a touring machine it will do 90 m.p.h. at full throttle.

I'm not a speed merchant, but ride fairly far in the day (occasionally 700 miles, often 500) and at a fair average, for the machine's speed in the open lets one crawl through the towns, and still average 40–42 miles in the hour. The riding position and the slow turn-over of the engine at speeds of 50-odd give one a very restful feeling.

There, it is no good telling you all you knew before I did. They are the jolliest things on wheels.

A delightful summing-up, and note his reference to 'your controls and designs'. Note there is no reference to any design by the writer of the letter and very pertinent to what we noted five paragraphs earlier.

This eulogy will be familiar to those fortunate enough to possess certain catalogues in which it appears, and it is also included in the *Letters of T. E. Lawrence*, edited by David Garnett. It is the reasoned writing of a matured and serious mind with no hint of excessive speed, and was obviously unknown to a contributor in a very daily newspaper not long ago (early 1963) who sneered at Lawrence as being a ton-up kid!

Many readers have read Lawrence's last work, published post-humously, *The Mint*, containing as it does one of the most vivid descriptions of a motor-cycle ride. Originally it appeared in the British Legion *Journal* for November 1933, which later I sent to the manufacturer for, as I anticipated, his great enjoyment. Here, for the benefit of those to whom the essay may be new, is this master-piece of descriptive writing from the *Journal*:

The extravagance in which my surplus emotion expressed itself lay on the roads. So long as roads were tarred blue and straight; not hedged; and empty and dry, so long was I rich.

Nightly I'd run up from the hangar upon the last stroke of work, spurring my tired feet to be nimble. The very movement refreshed them, after the day-long restraint of service.

In five minutes my bed would be down, ready for the night; in four more I was in breeches and puttees, pulling on my gauntlets as I walked over to my bike, which lived in a garage-hut opposite. Its tyres never wanted air, its engine had a habit of starting at second kick—a good habit, for only by frantic plunging upon the starter pedal could my puny weight force the engine over the seven atmospheres of its compression.

Boanerges' first glad roar at being alive again nightly jarred the huts of Cadet College into life. 'There he goes, the noisy beggar', someone would say enviously in every flight. It is part of an airman's profession to be knowing with engines: and a thoroughbred engine is our undying satisfaction. The camp wore the virtue of my Brough like a flower in its cap. Tonight Tug and Dusty came to the step of our hut to see me off.

'Running down to Smoke, perhaps?' jeered Dusty; hitting at my regular game of London and back for tea on Wednesday afternoons.

Boa is a top-gear machine, as sweet in that as most single-cylinders in middle. I chug most lordly past the guard-room and through the speed limit at no more than sixteen. Round the bend past the farm, and the way straightens. Now for it. The engine's final development is fifty-two horse-power. A miracle that all this docile strength waits behind the one tiny lever for the pleasure of my hand.

Another bend: and I have the honour of one of England's straightest and fastest roads. The burble of my exhaust unwound like a long cord behind me. Soon my speed snapped it, and I heard only the cry of the wind which my battering head split and fended aside.

The cry rose with my speed to a shriek; while the air's coldness streamed like two jets of iced water into my dissolving eyes. I screwed them into slits, and focused my sight two hundred yards ahead of me on the empty mosaic of the tar's gravelled undulations.

Like arrows the tiny flies pricked my cheeks: and sometimes a heavier body, some house-fly or beetle, would crash into face or lips like a spent bullet. A glance at the speedometer: seventy-eight. Boanerges is warming up.

I pull the throttle right open, on the top of the slope, and we swoop flying across the dip, and up-down-up-down the switchback beyond: the weighty machine launching itself like a projectile with a whirr of wheels into the air at the take-off of each rise, to land lurchingly with such a snatch of the driving chain as jerks my spine like a rictus.

Once we so fled across the evening light, with the mellow sun on my left, when a Bristol Fighter, from Whitewash Villas, our neighbouring aerodrome, was banking sharply round. I checked speed an instant to wave: and the slipstream of my impetus snapped my arm and elbow astern, like a raised flail.

The pilot pointed down the road towards Lincoln. I sat hard in the saddle, folded back my ears, and went away after him, like a dog after a hare. Quickly we drew abreast, as the impulse of his dive to my level exhausted itself.

The next mile of the road was rough. I braced my feet into the rests, thrust with my arms, and clenched my knees on the tank till its rubber grips goggled under my thighs. Over the first pot-hole Boanerges screamed in surprise, its mudguard bottoming with a yawp on the tyre. The plunges of the next ten seconds would have distinguished a kangaroo dodging gunfire. I clung on, wedging my gloved hand in the throttle lever so that no bump should close it and spoil our speed.

Then the bicycle wrenched sideways into three long ruts: it swayed dizzily wagging its tail for thirty awful yards. Out came the clutch, the engine raced freely; Boa checked and straightened his head with a shake as a Brough should.

The bad ground was passed and on the new road our flight became birdlike. My head was blown out with air so that my ears had failed and we seemed to whirl soundlessly between the sun-gilt stubble fields. I dared, on a rise, to slow imperceptibly and glance sideways into the sky.

There the Bif was, two hundred yards and more back. Play with the fellow? Why not? I slowed to ninety: signalled with my hand for him to overtake. Slowed ten more: sat up. Over he rattled. His passenger, a helmeted and goggled grin, hung out of the cockpit to pass me the 'Up yer' Raf randy greeting.

They were hoping I was a flash in the pan, giving them best. Open went my throttle again. Boa crept level, fifty feet below; held them; sailed ahead into the clean and lonely country. An approaching car pulled nearly into its ditch at the sight of our race.

The Bif was zooming among the trees and telegraph poles, with my scurrying spot only eight yards ahead. I gained though, gained steadily: was perhaps five miles an hour the faster. Down went my left hand to give the engine two extra dollops of oil, for fear that something was running hot: but an overhead Jap twin, supertuned like this one, would carry on to the moon and back unfaltering.

We drew near the settlement. A long mile before the first houses I closed down and coasted to the crossroads by the hospital. Bif caught up, banked climbed and turned for home, waving to me as long as he was in sight. Fourteen miles from camp, we are, here: and fifteen minutes since I left Tug and Dusty at the hut door.

I let in the clutch again and eased Boanerges down the hill along the tram-lines through the dirty street and up-hill to the aloof cathedral, where it stood in frigid perfection above the cowering close. No message of mercy in Lincoln. Our God is a jealous God: and man's very best offering will fall disdainfully short of worthiness, in the sight of St Hugh and his angels.

Remigius, earthy old Remigius, looks with more charity on me and Boanerges. I stabled the steel magnificence of strength and speed at his west door and went in: to find the organist practising something slow and rhythmical, like a multiplication table in notes, on the organ. The fretted, unsatisfying and unsatisfied lace-work of choir screen and spandrels drank in the main sound. Its surplus spilled thoughtfully into my ears.

By then my belly had forgotten its lunch, my eyes smarted and streamed. Out again to sluice my head under the White Hart's yard-pump. A cup of real chocolate and a muffin at the teashop: and Boa and I took the Newark road for the last hour of daylight. He ambles at forty-five and when roaring his utmost surpasses the hundred.

A skittish motor-bike with a touch of blood in it is better than all the riding animals on earth, because of its logical extension of our faculties, and the hint, the provocation, to the success conferred by its honeyed untiring smoothness. Because Boa loves me he gives me five more miles of speed than a stranger would get from him.

At Nottingham I added sausages to the bacon which I'd bought at Lincoln: bacon so nicely sliced that each rasher meant a penny. The solid pannier bags behind the saddle took all this and at the next stop (a farm) took also a felt hammocked box of fifteen eggs. Home by Sleaford, our squalid, purse-proud local village. Its butcher had six penn'orth of dripping ready for me. For months have I been making an evening round a'market-ing, twice a week, riding a hundred miles for the joy of it and picking up the best food cheapest, over half the countryside.

The fire is a cooking fire, red between the stove bars, all its flame and smoke burned off. Half past eight. The other ten fellows are yarning in a blue haze of tobacco, two on the chairs, eight on the forms, waiting my return. After the clean night air their cigarette smoke gave me a coughing fit. Also the speed of my last whirling miles by lamp-light (the severest test of riding) had unsteadied my legs so that I staggered a little. 'Wo-ups dearie', chortled Dusty. It pleases them to imagine me wild on the road. To feed this flight vanity I gladden them with details of my scrap against the Bif.

'Bring any grub?' at length enquires Nigger, whose pocket is too low, always, for Canteen. I knew there was something lacking. The excitement of the final dash and my oncoming weariness had chased from my memory the stuffed panniers of the Brough. Out into the night again steering across the black garage to the corner in which he is stabled by the fume of hot iron rising from his sturdy cylinders. Click, click, the bags are detached; and I pour out their contents before Dusty, the hut pantryman. Tug brings out the frying-pan and has precedency. The fire is just right for it. A sizzle and a filling smell. I get ready my usual two slices of buttered toast.

All of which illustrates how ignorant and feeble is the effort of the foreigner who referred to Lawrence and 'a motor-cycle'!

There seems to be some little doubt as to whether all the relevant facts about the accident which caused his death were ever clearly made known. Certainly much nonsense has been published and screened. George Brough himself has added to my knowledge the following: Lawrence was riding quietly through the Dorset country-side near Clouds Hill, when he was about to pass and overtake a butcher's boy on a bicycle accompanied by a cyclist friend on his inside. The boy, attracted apparently by the burble of the approaching big vee engine, glanced backwards and inadvertently swerved to-wards the centre of the road. As George put it: 'Like the perfect gentleman that he was, Lawrence banked over to miss the boy and

Mont Batten
Plymouth

27. 1. 31

Dear G. B.

I cannot answer your M/C correspondent direct, as I don't know who he is! So will you please thank him very much, and say that I come up to London only once a blue moon, and February's moons are all the colour of cream cheese?

It was very good of him to suggest it : but I wasn't ever officially a despatch-rider, and I'd feel rather out of it at a show like that. I have not been to any public dinners, either.

The '100 goes like stink, still. All its pristine manners came back to it, and it seems to me the best thing I have ever ridden. The tank is still whole and shining, tell me. Only I use the poor thing too little. There is a writing job to be finished this spring, after dragging over me for years + years. Perhaps by June I shall be free unless they hold a Schneider Cup in spite of all. Heaven forbid for my bike's sake.

The worst of Afghan Hounds is their hind legs, which are fitted with castor action: good for climbing mountains, but ridiculous on the flat. You will have to live in the Peak, to give the poor beast sport.

Yours
T E Shaw.

87   *A specimen of Colonel T. E. Lawrence's handwriting*

88 Colonel T. E. Lawrence and the maker together at Haydn Road

struck the offside verge. He was doing no more than 25 m.p.h. at that time, so it is perfectly possible that if he'd overruled his gentlemanly instinct and "taken" the cyclist, neither would have sustained anything worse than bruises and a shaking up.' I feel there is no more to add.

It is due to George's kindness that in Fig. 87 I am able to reproduce a hitherto unpublished letter he received from T. E. Lawrence dated 27 January 1931, as I am sure many readers may never have seen a sample of this great man's handwriting. Lawrence's reference to Afghan hounds is to *Zada*, Mr and Mrs Brough's beautiful pet of this breed which graced the precincts of Pendine at that time. It was a dog of great character. I cannot resist including in Fig. 88 the familiar but nevertheless appropriate photograph of Lawrence and George together, a happy occasion when Lawrence was leaving the old Haydn Road Works on a new SS100.

To conclude this chapter and to provide a contrast I must relate an occasion of ultra-slow-speed touring. It is not usual to associate motor-cycles with mountain climbing, although Snowdon and much of Ben Nevis have been ascended by motor-cycle at one time or another. But the most daring climb was made of Mount Merapi (7,500 feet), an extinct volcano in Java, by F. Sluymers on his SS80 in 1927. In the crater is Lake Kawa Idgar accessible only on foot or pony up the only mountain path 18 miles long. The ascent took two days. On the first day Sluymers put in 12 hours' climbing in low gear completing the climb after 5 hours during the second day, again in low gear, giving an average of just over one mile per hour. A most remarkable achievement remembering the steady decrease in atmospheric pressure on the carburettor as the elevation increased, a feat never repeated.

CHAPTER X

Here and There

In this penultimate chapter it is my intention to deal with several items which, although mentioned previously, can be covered in some detail more suitably when considered apart from the rest of the text. These observations must of necessity be rather brief.

One may say the vee engine and the Brough Superior are inseparables, we seldom think of one without thinking of the other, and therefore I feel a few notes on the origin and characteristics of the vee engine here may not be out of place. The vee engine has a long history, the earliest example recorded known to the author being that made by Messrs Carlsund in 1852 for a steam vessel. The cylinders, $24'' \times 36''$, were arranged at 90°. By the 1870's small steam vee twins were being produced and developed for propelling smaller vessels, the vee arrangement fitting nicely athwartwise in the hull. Usually the double-acting cylinders were at 90° with the big ends side by side on the same crankpin. One such engine built in 1867 with cylinders $4\frac{1}{4}'' \times 6''$ by a Norfolk firm is preserved in the Bridewell Museum, Norwich. Further prototype examples by other makers powered barges on canals and inland waterways. A variation was the inverted vee engine, naturally with the crankshaft on top. One, designed by D. & G. Thomson of Glasgow in the 1850's, had cylinders $41'' \times 36''$ and was fitted in the S.S. *Bordeaux*.

As the vee type fitted naturally into a ship's hull so did it later fit just as conveniently into the cycle frame of the period, and in so adapting this form of engine the early motor-cycle makers adopted therefore a well-proven layout. As some readers know a vee twin Norton won the heavyweight class in the first T.T. in 1907. For use in a motor-cycle however the cylinder angle was narrowed to—usually—50° which became, one might say, almost the standard angle. Phelon & Moore Ltd and Premiers preferred 90° in their examples prior to the first world war, Guzzi's placed their cylinders at 120° in 1935, J.A.P. at 50° (60° for the 1,100 c.c.) and Anzani used 57° at one time. 50° however became the common angle in other makes also.

The over-riding consideration is one of balance. In most single-cylinder engines it is usual to balance the main reciprocating parts by a weight attached to the crank webs or flywheels thus eliminating primary out-of-balance forces. Unfortunately the balance weight itself at its two extreme horizontal positions, i.e. when at right angles to the vertical centre-line of the engine, sets up its own out-of-balance forces known as secondary forces and of course, these occur horizontally twice each revolution. Treating the problem mathematically it can be shown that starting with two cylinders at 60° the unbalanced secondary vertical force increases as we decrease this angle of 60°, and decreases as we increase this angle towards 90°. Therefore if now we add another cylinder and gear at right-angles to the first cylinder making in effect a 90° twin, we eliminate the primary and secondary vertical and horizontal forces as they cancel each other out. All that remains is a relatively insignificant unbalanced secondary force whose extent or magnitude is the same in both vertical and horizontal planes. It is due to the obliquity of the connecting rods, and were we able to use connecting rods of infinite length the secondary force would disappear and perfect balance would result. Usually the bob or balance weight is fixed diametrically opposite the crankpin and should counteract the weight of the crankpin, the two connecting rods and that portion of the crank webs which is unbalanced. Where the big ends are mounted side by side on the crankpin, a twisting couple is imposed on the crankshaft which is absent when using a blade and forked rods because the centre of loading is through the centre of the pin. Thus the J.A.P., A.M.C. and Barr & Stroud designs have no twisting couple.

Both the single-cylinder and vertical twin engines with both crankpins arranged together are unbalanced, not only for primary but for secondary forces; so viewed from the dynamic standpoint, one has little or no advantage over the other.

By narrowing the angle to 50° a slightly heavier balance weight is required resulting in a small amount of primary unbalance. Nevertheless the result is an engine of far better balance than single or parallel twin. That the vee-twin motor-cycle has vanished from the English market is something that always staggers me, and indeed, all other big-twin enthusiasts. The sneaking suspicion comes to mind that English manufacturers must have forgotten how, and lost the skill required to machine a crankcase to mount twin cylinders at the familiar angle. If this surmise be incorrect, then their excuse is probably the 'extra production cost involved'. How much we don't know.

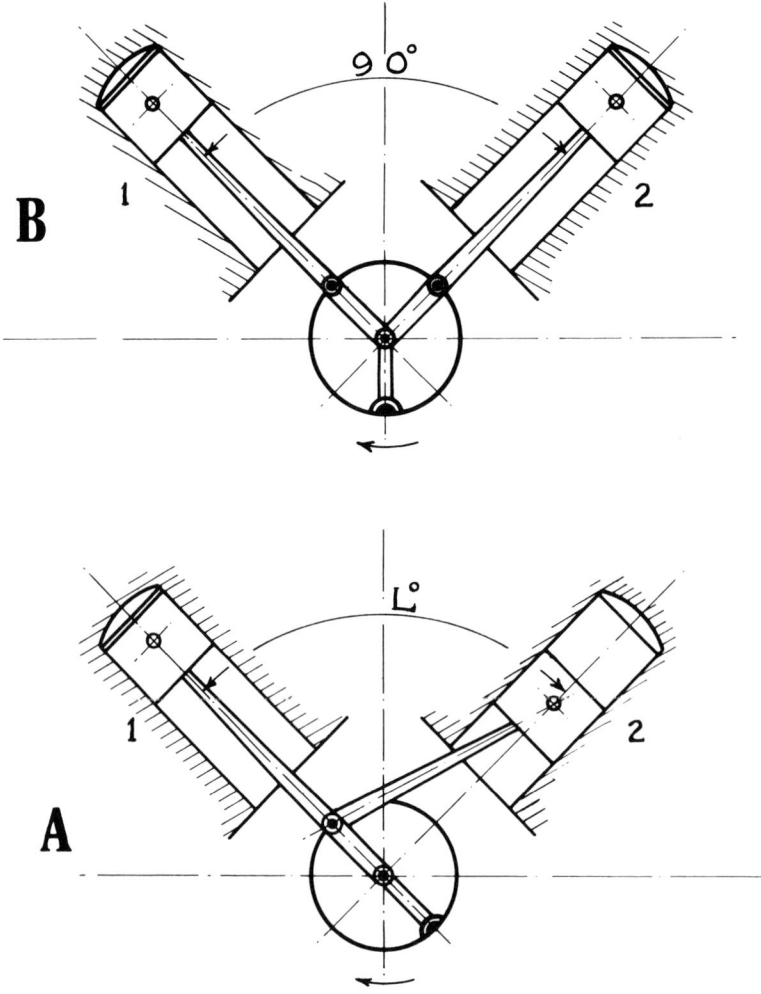

89 Firing diagrams for vee engines

What we do know is that so long as the present-day outlook is 'How cheap can we make it?', instead of 'Let us cater for every taste', then to England's lasting shame shall we have to go abroad for a vee twin in the middle of the twentieth century!

Reverting to the 90° vee twin we have seen that although the designer can achieve practically perfect balance, firing is uneven. Looking intently at the diagram in Fig. 89A and assuming No. 1 cylinder to fire, the crankpin rotates one complete revolution plus the included angle before No. 2 fires. After No. 2 has fired the crankpin has to rotate one revolution minus the included angle before No. 1 fires again. Or taking the first firing point as 0°, then No. 2 is at 360°+L, 360°−L and so on. For the standard 50° engine these points become 0, 410, 310, etc. For 90° the points become 0, 450, 270 and so on. To arrange for even firing twin cranks must be used as in the diagram in Fig. 89B, but this obviously upsets the excellent balance of the 90° engine. This will be seen to have a great bearing on what follows in the next paragraph.

During the last war, at Vernon Road an amount of development work on an entirely new 90° vee engine design was put in hand and strenuous efforts were made to find a compromise by which perfect balance and even firing could be obtained. Harold Karslake, released from the R.A.F. in 1943 to go to Vernon Road, evolved the ingenious 3-flywheel assembly depicted in Fig. 90, but even so the resultant uneven firing showed the finished engine to be little superior to the procurable types used hitherto. A complete bicycle was made and rigorously tested in 1944 as may be seen in Fig. 91. The different crankcase will be noticed at once, it being circular throughout, the flanges mounting the pushrod bases following A.M.C. SS100 practice. Cylinders, rocker covers with the BS monogram and the hairpin valve springs were also of A.M.C. origin. With more space available between the cylinders at 90° advantage was taken to place there the magdyno with the separate carburettors facing inwards, as seen in the illustration. The magdyno chain would have been totally enclosed of course in production models. Naturally the front and rear downtubes of the frame had to be splayed wider at the top (the wheelbase remained as on the SS100), requiring the battery to be placed in front of the crankcase with the oil tank a little above and behind the standard four-speed gearbox. Note the high-level exhaust pipes and silencers. It was, in short, a fine machine of great character.

Balancing a multiple vee engine is not all that simple either. If all connecting rods act on one long crankpin then there are uneven impulses between the working strokes; with 60° between the cylinders firing forces act at 60°, 300°, 60°, 300° and so on. Again, if the end throws are arranged at 120° from the centre throws in place of 180°, then no proper balance can be attained. Another scheme is to use only a two-throw crankshaft with the two front cylinders on one throw side by side or with forked and bladed rods, fitting the two rear cylinders to the other throw, and here the arrangement could be moderately well balanced by the addition of suitable weights on the

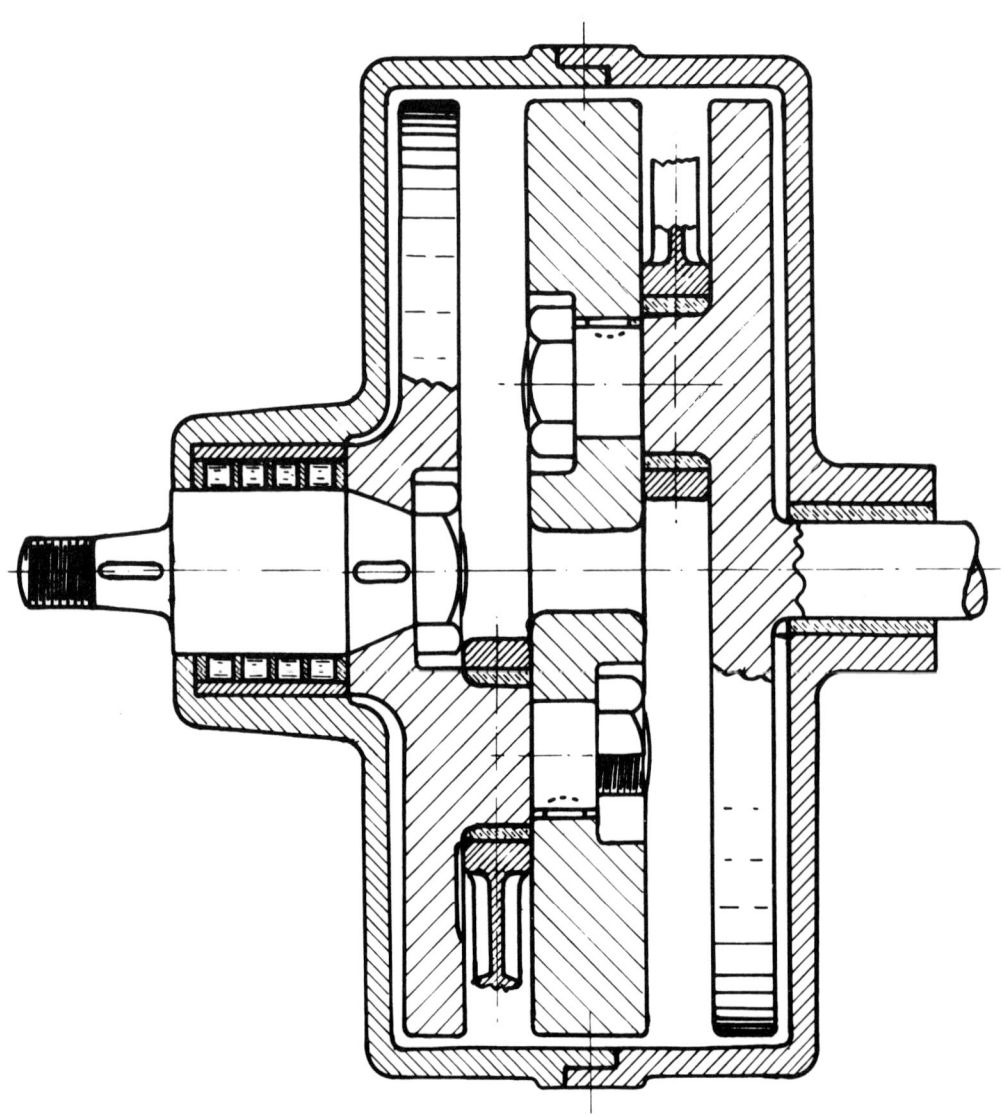

90   Harold Karslake's ingenious three-flywheel assembly for a 90° vee engine

91   The post-war 90° vee-twin machine—experimental only

flywheels, especially if the included angle is 90°, the angle between the two crankpins being a variable. But even firing unfortunately is not then possible. Placing the cranks at 180° with a 60° included cylinder angle produces firing intervals at 180°, 120°, 180°, 240° and so on, but with corresponding unequal suction impulses on the carburettor intake allowing probably one cylinder to be either too rich or too weak compared with the others. Lastly, using four throws on the shaft firing intervals occur at 120°, 240°, i.e. one interval is double the other. Good balance and even firing of a vee four is therefore a most difficult matter. This was discovered by designers many years ago when a vee-four engine was used in a steam wagon as early as 1902. Here the cylinders were at 90° with only two throws on the crankshaft, the camshaft being placed, as in the Brough Superior vee four, in the apex. So like the vee twin, the vee four is a type of engine of ancient lineage.

There is some little discrepancy in the published dimensions of the 1,100 c.c. J.A.P. engine. It has been stated the cylinders were 85·7 × 95 mm. in one journal and twice in another as 85 × 99 mm. and 85·7 × 104, the corresponding capacities being 1,095, 1,122 and 1,199 c.c. respectively. Obviously the first dimensions are correct. The 1,150 c.c. engine—so called—was the 1,100 c.c. engine in which the perpendicular depth of the cylinder heads was made $\frac{3}{64}''$ less, ($\frac{39}{64}''$ instead of $\frac{21}{32}''$), increasing the compression ratio a trifle. In

92 An existing steam-driven model ancestor of the modern vee engine

Appendix B will be found the leading dimensions of the engines
from Tottenham, and at one time fitted by George Brough as I feel
these data may prove helpful to many owners. In addition, Appendix
C contains b.h.p./speed curves for J.A.P. engines fitted, at one period
or another, in the Brough Superior.

Why is the vee twin popular with many people and what is the
secret of its fascination for me and others like me? I think the answer
is that the slightly irregular note of the vee-twin engine, especially at
low speeds, duplicates almost exactly the sound of a galloping horse,
so stimulating our minds to recognition of sounds familiar to our
ancestors over the centuries—sounds bred in us as it were, and
dormant. Certainly no other form of engine appeals so strongly to
some of us in this way.

93   The side-valve radial-three engine

Such is the fascination of the vee engine for me that some years ago I set about making a model of the prototype I previously referred to as being in the Bridewell Museum, Norwich, and I feel it appropriate to include a view of it in Fig. 92. Admittedly in this instance it is a steam engine but the ancestry, the drawing of the first lines may we say, has been done and so we see the cylinders at 90°, the outside flywheel, side-by-side connecting rods, the inlet pipe between the cylinders where it is today and, lastly, the downswept exhaust pipes. Even the valve gear is located to one side of the crankcase. It engenders a feeling of near-reverence when, divesting our minds of the self-satisfaction of the present, we compare the ancestor with the ultimate member of the family in Fig. 84.

With Messrs J. A. Prestwich's successors ceasing in 1963 to produce the 750 c.c. and 1,323 c.c. engines even for industrial purposes, it is indeed sad to reflect that now not one example of a vee twin is produced in this country, once the workshop of the world.

Before leaving the subject of engines, we must not omit reference to another engine developed towards the end of the last war, upon the recommendation of Granville Bradshaw. This was a radial three-cylinder with cylinders at 120°, the valves being of the flat disc type and rotated by vertical shafts in turn bevel-driven from the timing-gear chest. Compare its ancestor by William E. Brough already noticed in Fig. 4. In the later engine under consideration a port cut in the disc served to usher in the charge and after rotating the requisite amount, was ready to see its passage as exhaust, into the appropriate pipe. As in the earlier single-cylinder engine, trouble was experienced with distortion of the flat disc valves, although F. W. Stevenson and Harold Karslake spent much time and trouble running it in the works yard on a tripod using a propeller as an air brake.

However, another example was put in hand, but here the ordinary side valves took the place of the specials in the previous engine, and an idea of its interesting characteristics can be gleaned from the view of it in Fig. 93. The same two stalwarts spent some time on this engine rigged similarly to the first, but further development was not proceeded with.

Such an engine, with the requisite balance weight opposite the crankpin, possesses very good primary balance with no secondary couples if the connecting rods act on the crankpin in the same plane. If side by side on the crankpin, a slight secondary couple would result. Moreover it was a well-tried layout, and successful steam-driven examples had been on the market as early as 1888. My own opinion is that had it been possible to develop the side-valve version still further, its drive in a motor-cycle frame would have emulated the smoothness of a steam turbine, and the longitudinal crankshaft would have been ideal for arranging a final shaft drive.

All engineering firms who produced a standard product would in past, and I might say, happier times, produce unusual or non-standard machines to special order. The great variety of locomotives, road engines and the like testify to this so it is not surprising to find a number of unusual Brough Superiors left the works. We have room here for only a representative few, the first being *Moby Dick* which is probably known to most enthusiasts. Produced in 1929 as a spring-frame SS100, it was supplied to Mr C. R. Hobbs of Guildford and still bears the registration number TO 8878. Originally the compres-

94   A recent view of Moby Dick

sion ratio was 8 to 1, later increased to $8\frac{1}{2}$ to 1 when at the same time, under the supervision of Mr S. M. Greening at Tottenham, its capacity was increased to 1,123 c.c. In this form the big engine developed 57·5 b.h.p. at 5,000 r.p.m., returning 115·22 m.p.h. in top (5,200 r.p.m.), 109·21 in second gear with a ratio of 4·42 to 1. The large-bore twin-float Amal required a 375 jet. Further modifications were carried out again comprising two carburettors and a slight increase in capacity pushing the output up to a little over 65 b.h.p. Top gear was 3·5 to 1 but a lower ratio has been fitted to the low gear in the Sturmey-Archer box. Also, the wheelbase was made 3″ shorter than standard. Today it is a proud possession of Mr Thomas Eccles of Burnley and is illustrated in Fig. 94, showing the substitute tank of unusual shape. Valve timing is standard but ignition by a Bosch racing instrument occurs at 47° before top dead centre instead of 40°.

Then there was the Tottenham-engined works 'scrapper', as Ike Webb once described it to me, on which F. Dixon obtained a 5-mile sidecar record at 103 m.p.h. in 1927 and covered the Arpajon straight at 130 m.p.h., being the fastest kilometre one way. His average both ways was 129·1 m.p.h. During the next year the maker achieved 130·6 m.p.h. one way, being the then fastest speed in the

95 The works scrapper at Arpajon in 1928

world, and I make no excuse for illustrating in Fig. 95 a very familiar picture of it and the manufacturer on this occasion. 'The proudest day of my life' as he explained to me. It shows the compact lines of the record-breaker, its main features, and note how closely it resembled standard practice at that time. Experimental pistons on one occasion gave an amount of trouble, but this is expected in experimental work, and after slightly thicker crowns were used in another set, the trouble disappeared and George was able to gather in fourteen firsts at Doncaster, covering the half-mile rolling start at 100 m.p.h. He put up also a standing mile record at Pendine.

During the next year (1929) Herbert Le Vack returned 129·1 for the flying kilometre at Arpajon and the mile at 128 m.p.h. both ways. Reverting to Fig. 95 we see the engine resembled standard machines one could buy at that period and it was hand-built using mostly ordinary parts. The valves however were lightened and seated by three concentric springs, and the connecting rods were machined all over and polished. The final design of piston gave a compression ratio of 11 to 1, and with special Shell mixture the engine produced 60 b.h.p. at 6,000 r.p.m. Dixon suggested two carburettors back to

96 *Twin magnetos on the engine in Fig. 95*

back with guillotine throttle slides operated by rods and universal joints instead of Bowden cable. Twin float chambers to each instrument ensured ample feed under every condition. In addition to the ordinary top tank tube a square section tube was welded to the head lug and to the rear end of the top tube near the saddle, and contained an extra oil supply to the valve guides. All main fork members were stiffened and steel, not malleable, castings used. I was once privileged to sit on this masterpiece and what became apparent immediately was the feeling of 'oneness' with the machine.

In 1938 Mr M. N. Mavrogordato bought this famous bicycle from the maker and it enabled him to secure a Brooklands Gold Star and fastest time of the day at Syston, where he proved to be only one-fifth of a second slower than the course record previously set up by Eric Fernihough. The additional view of it in Fig. 96 shows the twin magnetos later fitted, the short wheelbase, not omitting the proud owner with whom it has permanently come to dwell.

Not all the unusual bicycles were built entirely for speed, as for example an SS100 produced in 1930 equipped with a Lucas dynamotor type A1000 11″ × 5″ supplied with current from a 12 v., 120-amp.-hour

*97 An SS80 with
near and offside
stabilisers*

battery housed in the sidecar locker. Connection to the crankshaft
was by a third chain in an oilbath, and when charging, the output
was eight ampères at 20 m.p.h. The headlamp bulb was of 36 watts,
sidecar 6 watts and 3 watts for the tail and these were all balanced
at 18 m.p.h. Incidentally when switched to start the motor would spin
the big engine when cold, the outfit being designed for a partially
disabled customer.

Again, there was the 1928 SS100, nickel-plated all over for a South
American customer who had to pay £230 for this unusual but none-

138

the-less impressive finish. So one could go on covering many pages, but I am afraid these few examples must suffice.

However, owners were at liberty to alter and modify their machines as they pleased and two notable modifications are worth recording.

The first is illustrated in Fig. 97 and took the form of near- and off-side stabilisers fitted to a solo SS80. Both the side mudguards were reinforced so that two passengers besides the rider and pillionist or four altogether, could be carried. It required some alteration to the silencers which were arranged as may be seen in the end view. Although looking rather heavy the cleading was of aluminium sheet and the framing a light steel structure.

A successful Brough Superior rider in the classic trials was F. W. Stevenson, for many years at the Main Street Garage, Bulwell and still happily active. His modification was to incorporate a sidecar wheel drive illustrated in the views shown in Fig. 98, where it will be seen the ordinary rear forks have been replaced with two $\frac{3}{8}''$ triangular steel plates braced together, and between them is a phosphor-bronze housing containing a self-aligning ball bearing and a ball thrust bearing. The rear wheel is carried on a spindle through these bearings enabling it to be located on a 3-stud fixing and therefore easily removable. The phosphor-bronze housing incidentally is pivoted on a

98   F. W. Stevenson's design of sidecar wheel drive

bottom bolt and can be moved fore and aft for chain adjustment. The sidecar chassis of ordinary tubular construction can be seen in the illustrations including the extended shaft carrying the Enfield cush-drive chain wheel and at its far end the sidecar wheel. An 8″ internally expanding brake is incorporated in the rear wheel in the usual way and an 8″ externally contracting brake on the rear shaft. In addition, a dog clutch controlled by a handle enables the sidecar wheel to be put out of drive if necessary. Cee-springs carrying the body however are reversed in this case.

Advantages claimed for this device are easier cornering and that the two-wheel drive enables more use to be made of the power from the big side-valve engine. Stevenson, in 1933–4, won the Trier's Cup in the Cotswold, made best sidecar performance in the Bemrose and won the unlimited sidecar award in the Travers Trials with this outfit.

Some of the early sidecars were made by the Tornado Manufacturing Company, Weybridge. Sir William Lyons, today of Jaguar Cars, once raced Brough Superiors in the days when his small firm was Lyons & Walmsley in Bloomfield Road, Blackpool. His first sidecar appeared in 1922, the body being made in Blackpool but mounted on a Montgomery chassis. Most had octagonal panels of polished aluminium, and one of them attached to a '90 Bore' with Montgomery forks forms the delightful combination seen already in Fig. 16. This model was usually called the *Coupé de Luxe*. In 1924 some were pentagonal and listed at £22 10s. One such was exhibited on the Brough Superior stand at Olympia in 1923 when they were known as Swallow sidecars; the Swallow Sidecar Company having been floated in 1920 with a working capital of only £1,000! Based on sound design and quality they continued production until the outbreak of the Second World War. In 1927 the Nottingham police bought a series of Brough Superiors fitted with Swallow sidecars.

A few extra notes about the famous bulbous-nosed Brough Superior saddle tanks may prove interesting to many readers. Made originally in Nottingham, of Staybrite steel, the nose ends were first hand-beaten to shape and then smoothed in a rolling machine. After bending the sides the nose was fitted by hand soldering, the joint being tacked first for lining up and then the whole seam finished. No jigs or formers were used for the final assembly, it being remembered that each tank was made individually for the corresponding machine. The Brough Superior tank was plated over a greater area than those of contemporary other makes, which were usually enamelled all over. It was not until the *Black Alpine* appeared that this famous tank was enamelled all over, in eggshell black, lined with a thin gold or silver line where the plating would have met the ordinary enamelling. Early models had an oil compartment on the right-hand side requiring its own filler cap. After separate oil tanks were fitted, the twin filler caps were retained for the sake of symmetry.

Racing imposed stresses on tanks not easy to assess and thus as we have seen in Figs. 79 and 80 some racing tanks were secured by three bands instead of the usual four under-studs and nuts. Black and chrome was not the only colour used, and in one National Rally I saw an SS80 equipped with a tank finished in a deep purple-red, a shade darker than the familiar 'Midland Red' used on locomotives on the old Midland Railway.

It is not generally known that Colonel T. E. Lawrence specified stainless steel for his tank which was transferred to his successive machines. It proved rather difficult to make, there being much wastage of material in the process, and it was sent to Sheffield three times for annealing.

Two interesting late patents deserve some passing reference, viz. those sealed in the names of Ballamy, Sheepshanks and G.B. and listed in Appendix A.

In No. 562,686 of 1946 a new suspension system is involved. The bottom links of the forks oscillate in a box, each link having a bevel wheel on the end. This bevel meshes in turn with its corresponding bevel on the lower end of a torsion bar running within the fork tube. It is obvious that when the links move by virtue of road irregularities the torsion bar will twist to suit, thus absorbing the shocks. The top end of each torsion bar is held in a splined collar. The collars can rotate and are connected by a turnbuckle across the top of the steering column. Thus initial damping can be increased or decreased, depending upon which way the turnbuckle is screwed. Needless to say the lower bevel boxes work in oil. An identical layout would serve for the rear springing also.

The second patent is No. 564,317 of 1944 and covers the changing of gears in a three-speed box by oil. In this arrangement the driving-gear pinions are mounted on the crankshaft set across the frame. The secondary shaft is hollow and carries the corresponding three gears meshing with the first set. Now each driven gear wheel has its centre formed like a brake drum containing brake shoes mounted on the shaft. The centre of the secondary shaft, being hollow, contains a long plunger so drilled that oil from the pump can, according to the amount of movement given to the plunger by the handlebar control, expand the appropriate pair of shoes thus forming a rigid drive between the particular pair of geared wheels. In the neutral position the oil flows through an annular slot back to the sump without affecting any pair of shoes (i.e. wheels). A bleed pilot passage in the low-gear shoe's centre permits the drive to be taken up slowly. As the machine begins to move, the piston is moved a little further, sealing the bleed and giving full expansion to the shoes, i.e. full drive. Thus is the usual clutch dispensed with.

Altogether two extremely valuable and interesting patents, foreshadowing how progressive the post-war Brough Superiors could have been if ruling prices, at that time, had not made their manufacture—compatible with the maker's standard of quality—uneconomic.

Instead of motor-cycles, post-war work at Vernon Road has comprised the manufacture of almost every conceivable sort of precision part for the engineering industry. Complete test benches for testing the output and analysing the exhaust gases of small internal combustion engines have been made for Tecequipment Ltd, for use in technical colleges. Over 22,000 small engines have been produced for hand-controlled horticultural cultivating machines. Castings in all metals are machined to any fineness of limit and complexity. Even precision ground valve spindles for reciprocating steam engines have been made at one time and the extent is endless, and includes, of course, parts for Brough Superiors as replenishment of stocks becomes necessary. The works is always working to full capacity under the present management and guidance of George, ably supported by Mr Terence Ball, the present works director, who must also be known to many Brough owners and riders.

CHAPTER XI

Conclusion

The Brough Superior could not have been evolved, built and developed without a guiding personality at the head of affairs. Today, in a mechanical age, the humanities tend to be neglected and therefore it seems most fitting for me to conclude this volume with a short tribute to the man who made it all possible and real.

In a number of places on the preceding pages the reader will have caught glimpses of the character of the Designer-Rider-Manufacturer as some point or occasion has been described; his photograph has appeared in several illustrations, and we have noticed at the very beginning how he was riding to school at the tender age of twelve years. Many Brough Superior owners will be acquainted with most of what follows but the larger interested public is not so favoured. I once heard George described in motor-cycling company as the 'greatest all-rounder' and I think that is an ideal description. It covers riding in the T.T., winning more awards in the long-distance type of classic trial than any other maker, successfully lapping Brooklands' famous saucer when a young man and again in 1933 with a sidecar when aged forty-three, missing a Gold Star by 0·79 of a mile per hour, winning numerous sand races and attaining the 'world's fastest' distinction on one occasion. On *Old Bill* as I mentioned earlier he won 51 'firsts' out of 52 entries, and he 'confesses' to over 200 racing firsts altogether. A gold medal from the London–Edinburgh has been his 23 times at least, not to mention the Land's End, the *Motor Cycling* Cup and many other classic awards. By November 1922 he possessed 89 gold medals and 34 cups, and when aged thirty-five, the total was 200 and 70 respectively. High speed at Arpajon requires one brand of courage. Another brand is required to take a 6 h.p. (old rating) vee-twin Brough with a fixed belt drive in 1913 through the Scottish Six Days Trial. Not only did George finish the trial but as it totalled 980 miles, he asked official observers to witness an extra twenty to make up a round thousand! Samson, observer for *The Motor Cycle* did so. George Brough has both brands. It takes character too, to stand up to a magistrate when still at school, for

99 The Designer-Rider-Manufacturer on a recent happy occasion

riding without a licence and for speeding—and to parental censure afterwards. It takes faith to start one's own business and leadership to carry it on. George believed the best form of leadership in his position was to go out and win events whereby the staff, behind him to a man, eagerly awaited on Saturday evenings for results to see how the 'guvnor' had fared. Such directorship brought results in the business field too, enabling him to spare some thousands of pounds on developing new ideas—ideas which in practical form we have enjoyed studying in previous chapters. No doubt many more worldly goods would have come his way had he concentrated solely on just three types, say the SS100, SS80 and the o.h.v. 680, telling clients they could have any colour so long as it was black. But this a creative artist cannot do and so there appeared those several ideals translated into engineering form. An odd failure or two, that is life. Most were successful. What glorious successes!

Two important factors contributed I think to his successes. Firstly, he had an inborn gift of engineering knowledge, and later became a corporate member of the Institution of Automobile Engineers (now incorporated in the Institution of Mechanical Engineers). For example, George could take a glance at the outgoing flaming gases with the pipe removed and give one an uncannily accurate assessment of the state of the carburation. He needed to ride a machine but a very short distance to give an all-embracing opinion of its faults and credits, and the state of the engine, and so on. He had but to sit on a stationary bicycle in order to tell if everything was suitable, properly positioned and if it had the correct 'feel'.

Equally important was his gift of 'eye' for line and composition, and by a sixth sense he knew when a design looked right, when the position of something was wrong, or when it was correct. He knew precisely what was wanted, inspired his staff—and got it. An excellent example of and proof of his flair for 'line' is to be seen in the Frontispiece and in Fig. 53, where I pointed out it would be difficult to fault the position of any item or fitting. He was therefore able to embody lines and profiles making the Brough Superior as pleasing to the eye as it was potent in performance.

There are times when Fortune fails to favour us, and so we shall not be surprised to find he crashed his four-cylinder machine in 1932 in the neighbourhood of Lockerbie in avoiding a dog and spent some time following in Carlisle Hospital. Apparently the outfit overturned, breaking the sidecar connections. There were his accidents at Brooklands and Clipstone described in Chapter III and again in the I.S.D.T. when he sustained a broken leg and F. P. Dickson lost his life. Even today the after-effects have to be alleviated at a suitable spa on the Continent. Therefore I feel it most appropriate to include as a final and informal illustration in Fig. 99 the happy picture of George at one of the Brough Superior Club gatherings. These annual functions are neatly following a tradition instituted by the maker many years ago. It happened thus and is an example of yet another 'first'. Then in 1929, George invited all Brough owners to a rally-cum-field day at Chipping Norton, when he became host to over four hundred happy people at lunch in the Drill Hall. After this sumptuous affair the afternoon was spent in energetic sports and this function formed the first one-make rally ever held and organised by a manufacturer. The past repeats itself and so is future for in 1960 the Brough Superior Club proposed to hold its annual lunch and rally in Wollaton Park, Nottingham. George got to hear about it, and that if it rained the stalwarts would be without shelter. As he put it to me afterwards, 'I therefore got in touch with a tent maker and hired the largest size marquee it was possible to get. I had it properly staffed and the three-course lunch with wines and beer was laid on with my compliments to all the Brough Superior riders present. Incidentally the cost of this to me was one of the expenditures in my life that I have taken the greatest pleasure out of.' I was privileged to be there and can testify to it being one of my happiest days. It also illustrates a little of the maker's extremely generous side.

So today in the active and colourful autumn of his life he is regularly visited by past and present owners at the works and always attends annual meetings of the Club. It is then our privilege to have him move freely amongst us as it is his privilege and pleasure to know *he* is the cause of such a gathering of his fellow men—a pleasure and satisfaction no material riches could ever buy.

MEMORÆ   SACRVM
GEORGE BROUGH
BORN   21ST. APRIL 1890
DIED   12TH. JANUARY 1970

A List of Patents in the Names of those Associated with the Brough Superior

Ballamy/Sheepshanks. G.B. (Nottingham) Ltd

No. 562,686—Improvements in or relating to spring suspension devices for bicycles and like vehicles. Application 27 November 1942. Complete specification 8 December 1943. Accepted 12 July 1946. Leslie Mark Ballamy, Arthington, Harestone Hill, Caterham, Surrey. Richard Hasell Sheepshanks, Old Rookery House, Eyke, Suffolk. G.B. (Nottingham) Ltd., Grosvenor Chambers, 23 King Street, Nottingham.

No. 564,317—Improvements in or relating to change speed gear mechanism more particularly for vehicles. Application 18 February 1943. Complete specification 17 March 1944. Accepted 22 September 1944. Names as above.

Brough/Karslake

No. 16,389—Improvements in prop stands for cycles, motor-cycles and the like. Application 25 June 1925. Accepted 12 August 1926. George Brough and Harold Karslake, both of Brough Superior Works, Haydn Road, Nottingham.

No. 3941—Application in 1925. Became void.

No. 866—Application in 1926. Became abandoned.

Brough/Poppe

No. 126,927—A new and improved roller bearing for use with the crankshafts of internal combustion engines. Application 15 February 1919. Accepted 22 May 1919. George Brough, W. E. Brough & Co., Basford, Nottingham. Erling Poppe, 'Logna', Warwick Avenue, Coventry.

Brough, W. E.

No. 6523—Drag Shoe. Application in 1892.

No. 3696—Motor-powered engine. Application in 1896.

No. 9640—Stand or elevator. Application in 1897.

No. 4291—Self-propelled vehicles. Application in 1903.

No. 3721—Motor-car resilient springs. Application in 1906.

No. 24,324—Motor-car pneumatic springs. Application in 1906.

No. 21,737—Preventing vehicles side-slipping. Application in 1907.

No. 1634—Vehicle wheel rims. Application in 1908.

No. 27,570—Internal combustion engine valves. Application in 1909.

No. 7788—Vehicle wheels. Application in 1910.

No. 26,564—Splash guards. Application in 1913.

Burt, P., J. S. & T. W.

No. 8295—Internal combustion engines. 23 April 1901. P.

No. 13,652—Regulating internal combustion engines. 14 June 1906. P.

No. 18,140—Internal combustion engine. 6 August 1909. P.

No. 6569—Internal combustion engine. 16 March 1910. P., J. S. & T. W.

No. 23,953—Internal combustion engine. 17 October 1910. P., J. S. & T. W.

No. 25,438—Internal combustion engine valve mechanism. 2 November 1910. P.

No. 27,214—Cutting ports in engine cylinders. 23 November 1910. P.

No. 15,900—Valve actuating mechanism. 2 July 1910. J. S.

No. 7156—Starting internal combustion engines. 23 March 1912. P.

No. 26,261—Internal combustion engines. 15 November 1912. P.

No. 5683—I.C. engines. 7 March 1913. P.

No. 7879—I.C. engines. 3 April 1913. P.

No. 19,086—I.C. engines. 26 August 1914. P.

No. 10,304—I.C. engines. 15 July 1915. P.

No. 118,764—I.C. engines. J. S.

No. 123,578—I.C. engines. J. S.

No. 158,502—I.C. engines. P.

No. 156, 895—Connecting rods. P.

No. 137,779—I.C. engines. P.

No. 268,988—I.C. engines. P.

No. 456,120—I.C. engines. P.

No. 459,702—I.C. engines. P.

No. 459,704 Valve-operating mechanism for I.C. engines. P.

No. 438,994—I.C. engines. P.

No. 510,229—Cooling I.C. engines. T. W.

No. 516,668—I.C. engines. P.

No. 548,087—I.C. engines. P.

A. D. Draper

No. 9020—Lubricating engines. 11 April 1911. Alick Darby Draper, 4, Fenchurch Avenue, London, E.C.

No. 21,698—Lubricating engine. 2 October 1911.

No. 190,589—Anti-vibration devices for vehicles.

No. 191,588—Improvements in or relative to anti-vibration devices for use with springing devices. Application 14 December 1921. Accepted 18 January 1923.

No. 259,034—Motor-cycles—damping devices.

No. 259,401—Spring frames for cycles.

No. 260,774—Vehicle shock-absorber.

No. 293,664—Hydraulic shock-absorbers.

No. 293,941—Spring suspension systems.

No. 294,128—Anti-vibration devices.

No. 338,466—Hydraulic shock-absorbers.

No. 358,387—Anti-vibration devices for vehicles.

Adolf Felber

No. 413,239—Improvements in or relating to the construction of sidecar chassis for vehicles such as motor vehicles. Application 16 February 1934. Accepted 12 July 1934. Adolf Felber, 39 Arndtstrasse, Vienna xii, Austria.

McCallum, P. F., J. G. & J.

No. 7257—Internal combustion engines. 25 March 1898. P. F.

No. 22,610—Engines and pumps. 17 October 1902. P. F.

No. 17,513—Carburettors. 24 July 1914. J. G.

No. 182,840—Internal combustion engines. J.

No. 202,556—Internal combustion engines. J.

J. A. Prestwich & Co. Ltd.

No. 22135—Lubricating engines. Date, 1912.

Leading particulars of J.A.P. Engines fitted to the Brough Superior

Type	Bore m/m	Stroke m/m	Capacity c.c.	Height inches
1,100 s.v. 60°	85·7	95	1096	19
1,000 o.h.v. STD	80	99	995	22 7/16
1,000 Racing 8-45	85·7	85	980	21 7/16
1,000 Racing 8-50	80	99	995	22 7/16
1,000 Sports. s.v. 8-30	85·7	85	981	19 11/16
750 s.v. STD	70	97	747	16 5/8† 17 1/2‡
680 o.h.v. STD	70	88	674	20 11/16
680 s.v. STD	70	88	674	16 5/8
500 o.h.v. STD	60	88	498	20 1/16
500 Racing o.h.v.	62·5	80	490	20 7/16

Width inches	Length inches	Big end	Bearings Timing Side	Driving Side	Piston Rings No. × Width
13 1/2	19 1/4	RLR	Ball	Ball	4 × 3/16″
12 7/8* 10 1/4	20 1/4	RLR	RLR	RLR	3 × 1/4″
10 1/4	20 1/4	RLR	RLR	RLR	3 × 1/4″
12 7/8	20 1/4	RLR	RLR	RLR	3 × 3/16″
10 1/4	19 1/4	RLR	Ball	Ball	3 × 3/16″
11 5/8† 12 1/4‡	14 7/8† 15 1/2‡	RLR† RLR‡	Ph.Br† RLR‡	RLR† RLR‡	3 × 3/16″
12 1/4	18 1/4	RLR	Ph.Br.	RLR	3 × 3/16″
11 1/2	14 7/8	RLR	Ph.Br	RLR	3 × 3/16″
12 1/4	18	RLR	Ph.Br	RLR	3 × 3/16″
13	18 1/4	RLR	RLR	RLR	3 × 1/4″

Top Gear	Compression Ratio	Volume c.c.	Weight lb.	B.H.P.	At R.P.M.
4·75	4·7	147	124	28·5	4600
3·5	6·4	108	126	43·7	4800
3·25	8·1	87	110	45	4500
3·25	10	55	126	57	5500
3·5	5·2	117	106	34	4500
4·5	5·5† / 5‡	83† / 93‡	68† / 90‡	18·8† / 18·57‡	4000† / 3800‡
4·25	6·8	58	84	25	4500
4·5	5·2	80	68	17½	4000
4·25	6·1	49	98	19·2	4400
4	8·5 / 10·0 / 11·3	33 / 27 / 22	99	31·4	5000

TIMING					
Inlet opens Before t.d.c.	Inlet closes After b.d.c.	Exhaust opens before b.d.c.	Exhaust closes After t.d.c.	Magneto Before t.d.c.	Symbol
25°–$\frac{13}{64}$″	65°–$\frac{11}{16}$″	65°–$\frac{11}{16}$″	25°–$\frac{13}{64}$″	38°–$\frac{1}{4}$″	LTZ
15°	60°	63°	23°	45°	JTO
15°–$\frac{1}{32}$″	60°–$\frac{11}{16}$″	62½°–$\frac{7}{8}$″	22½°–$\frac{1}{16}$″	40°–$\frac{7}{16}$″	KTOR
15°	60°	63°	23°	45°	JTOR
15°–$\frac{7}{64}$″	60°–$\frac{11}{16}$″	62½°–$\frac{11}{16}$″	22½°–$\frac{1}{16}$″	40°–$\frac{7}{16}$″	KTCY KTCS KTR
18°	45°	60°	25°	35°† 40°‡	MT
23°	63°	65°	25°	45°	GTO
18°	45°	60°	25°	40°	GT
20°	50°	50°	20°	40°	YTO
20°	65°	65°	25°	45°	PTOR

* Bevel Magneto Drive. † One-piece cylinders with valve caps up to 1934.
‡ Detachable heads and enclosed valve box. After 1934.
Note—Some timing events could vary slightly for tuning purposes.

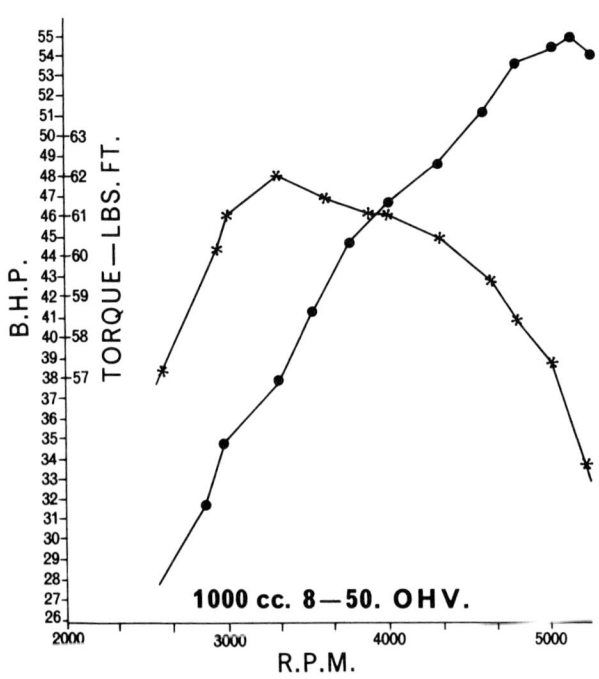

1000 cc. 8—50. OHV.

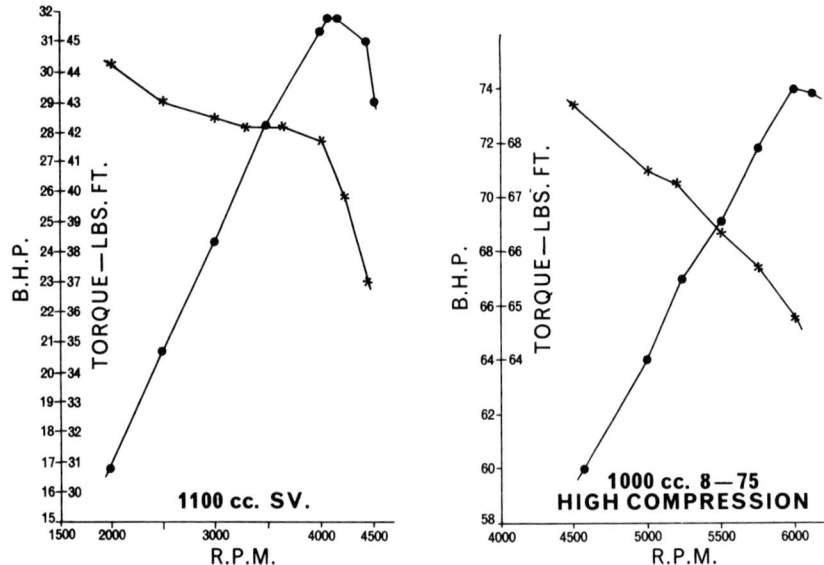

1100 cc. SV.

1000 cc. 8—75
HIGH COMPRESSION

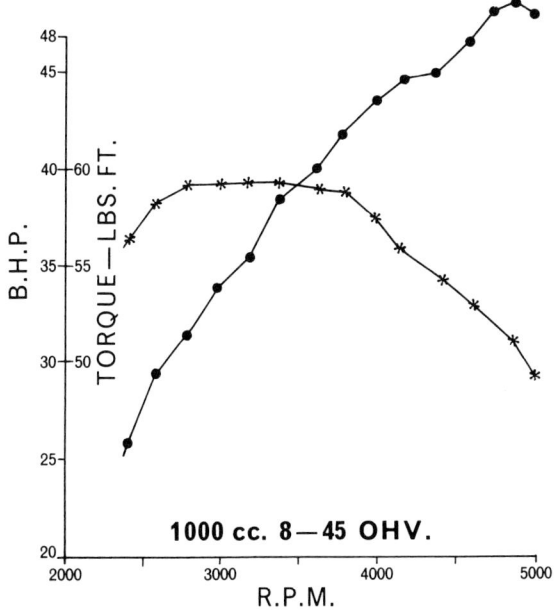

1000 cc. 8—45 OHV.

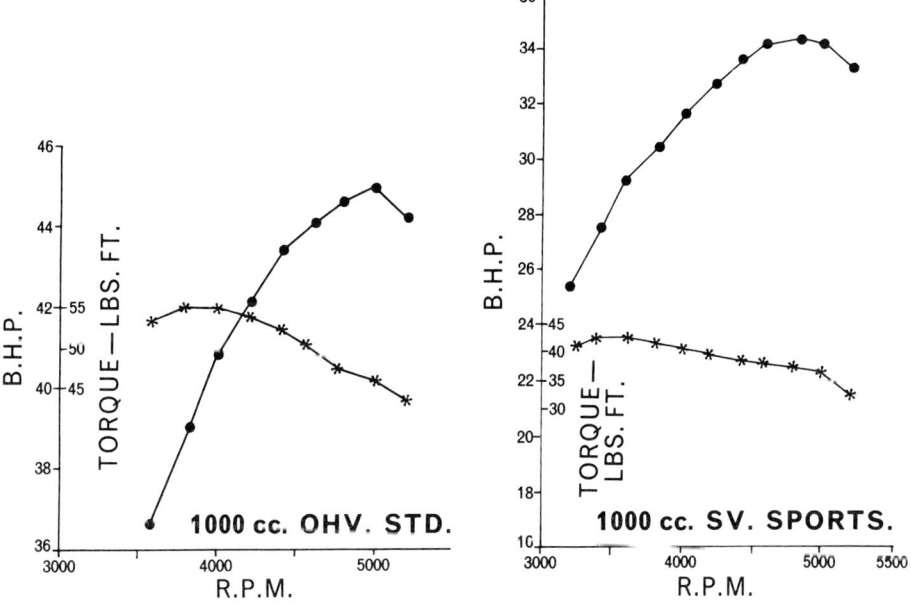

1000 cc. OHV. STD.

1000 cc. SV. SPORTS.

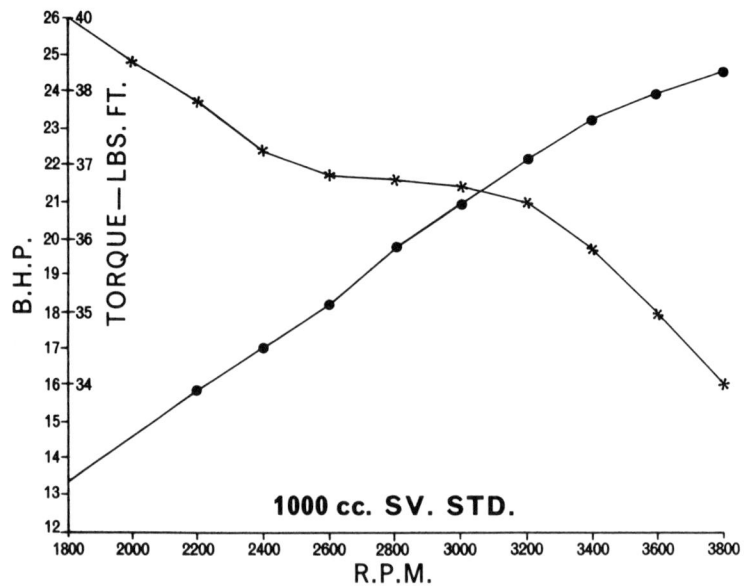

1000 cc. SV. STD.

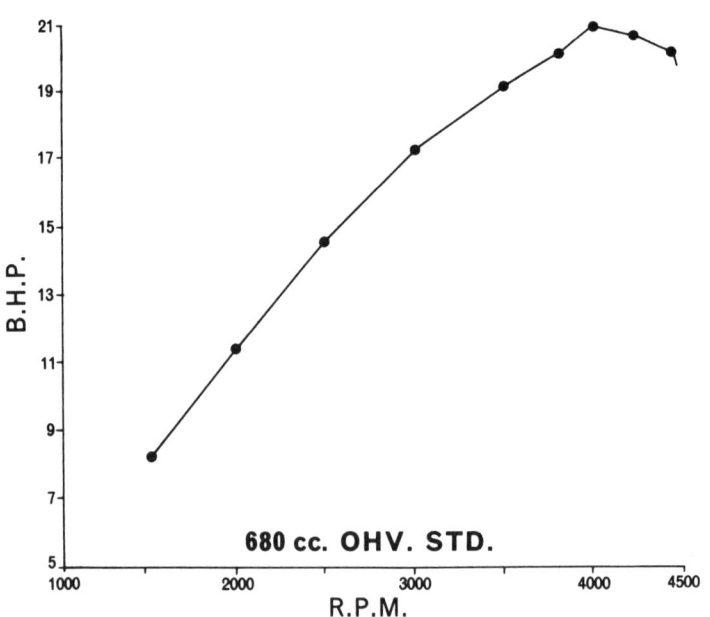

680 cc. OHV. STD.

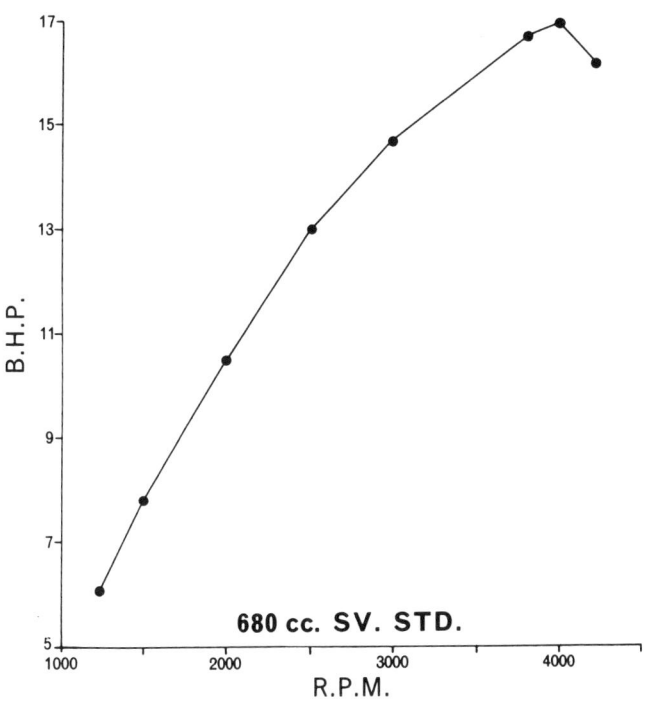

680 cc. SV. STD.

APPENDIX D
Some particulars of A.M.C. (Matchless) Engines

Type	Inlet opens	Inlet closes	Exhaust opens	Exhaust closes	Magneto	Plug points	Jets	Slide	Tappets-Inlet	Tappets-Exhaust
SS80	$\frac{3}{64}''$ 15° Before T.D.C.	$\frac{33}{64}''$ 52° After B.D.C.	$\frac{19}{32}''$ 55° Before B.D.C.	$\frac{1}{32}''$ 12½° After T.D.C.	$\frac{7}{32}''$* Gap ·012″	·018″	170	6/3	·003″ hot	·004″ hot
SS100	$\frac{1}{16}''$ 21° Before T.D.C.	$\frac{33}{32}''$ 60° After B.D.C.	$\frac{37}{64}''$ 56° Before B.D.C.	$\frac{5}{32}''$ 23° After T.D.C.	$\frac{3}{8}''$ Gap ·012″	·020″	170 to 180	9/4	Just clear cold	Just clear cold

* Usually $\frac{3}{16}''$ when a sidecar is fitted.

155

A brief list of some of the many successes achieved by Brough Superiors over the years

1921

A.C.U. Eastern Midlands Championship Trial. Championship Cup and Gold Medal.

Land's End—H. Karslake, Gold Medal.

Edinburgh—H. Karslake, Gold Medal.

Land's End—S. W. Ratcliffe, Silver Medal.

A.C.U. Championship—Cup for best performance by a Derby Club member.

Nuneaton Hill Climb—Captain J. A. Watson-Bourne, 1st and f.t.d.

Pendine Sands, 2½-mile sprint—Handel-Davies, 1st.

Newport and District Hill Climb—Handel-Davies, two firsts and one second.

Blaenavon and District Hill Climb—E. R. Richards, 1st.

Aberdare Club Cup Trial—E. R. Richards, full marks.

Scottish Six Days—George Brough, Gold Medal.
                    Harold Karslake, Gold Medal.

London–Exeter—J. D. Marvin, Gold Medal.

1922

Land's End—J. D. Marvin, Gold Medal.

B.M.C.R.C.—J. D. Marvin, Senior Passenger Handicap.

London–Exeter—J. D. Marvin, Gold Medal.

Yorkshire Centre Trial—Captain J. Watson-Bourne, Silver Cup.

Coventry and Warwickshire Championship Trial—Captain J. Watson-Bourne, Championship Cup and Gold Medal.

Midland Centre A.C.U. Trial—Captain J. Watson-Bourne, Gold Medal.

A.C.U. Six Days Trial—Captain J. Watson-Bourne, Gold Medal.

Bournemouth Hill Climb—J. Caslake, Jun., f.t.d. solo and sidecar.

Leinster 51-mile race—N. P. Metcalf, 54 min. 34 sec. and fastest lap.

Broomlu Cup Trial—S. Wallace, Gold Medal.

Jaffe Cup Trial—S. Wallace, Jaffe Cup.

1923

Croydon S.E. Centre Hill Climb—B. S. Allen, f.t.d. solo and sidecar.

Brighton Open Speed Trials—B. S. Allen, f.t.d. and three firsts.

Kent & Surrey Club Hill Climb—B. S. Allen, f.t.d. solo and sidecar.

Farncombe Hill, Brighton—B. S. Allen, f.t.d.

Worthing Speed Trials—B. S. Allen, f.t.d.

Bristol Club Hill Climb, 1,000 c.c. class—B. S. Allen, 1st.

Rochester Hill Climb—B. S. Allen, f.t.d.

Bradford M.C.C. Hill Climb—A. Greenwood, Dyson 100-guinea Shield, 2 Silver Cups.

Yorkshire Centre Speed Event—A. Greenwood, f.t.d. solo and sidecar.

East Midland A.C.U. Speed Trial, Gainsborough—A. Greenwood, f.t.d.

Stalybridge Hill Climb—A. Greenwood, f.t.d. solo and sidecar. Record for course.

Colmore Cup Trial—Jack Montgomery, Gold Medal.

Manville Trophy Trial—Jack Montgomery, Special Gold Medal. Best sidecar performance.

Coventry 'Golden Goblet' Trial—Jack Montgomery, *Motor Cycle* Cup, Gold Medal.

Bournemouth Hill Climb—J. Caslake, Jun., f.t.d. sidecar.

Southampton and District M.C.C. Hill Climb—J. Caslake, Jun., f.t.d. solo and sidecar.

Salisbury M.C.C. Hill Climb, J. Caslake, Jun., f.t.d., solo and sidecar.

Southampton M.C.C. Hill Climb—J. Caslake, Jun., f.t.d. sidecar.

Leinster 100—N. P. Metcalf, 1st 200-guinea Cup.

Irish 50 Race—N. P. Metcalf, Fastest lap, $4\frac{3}{4}$ miles in 4 min. 64 secs.

Ulster M.C.C.—S. Wallace, Gold Medal.

Brooklands—H. Le Vack, 200 miles solo, 1st. 200 miles sidecar, 1st. Also seven world's records: 1 hour and 200 miles solo, 50, 100, 200 miles and 1 hour and 2 hours records. 2-laps Scratch Race, 1st. 2-laps Scratch Sidecar Race, 1st.

1924

Arpajon—H. Le Vack, flying kilo 119·0 m.p.h. solo; flying mile 118·9 m.p.h. solo; flying kilo 99·8 m.p.h. sidecar; flying mile 99·7 m.p.h. sidecar.

London–Edinburgh—fifteen starters—fifteen Gold Medals.

Land's End—Three Gold Medals.

Pendine, Welsh T.T.—T. Spann, 1st.

Grand Prix of Baden (Austria) 100-kilo Race—Archduke Wilhelm Hapsburg, 1st.

1925

Pendine, Welsh T.T.—T. Spann, 1st.

Records for the following courses: Doncaster, Stalybridge, Saltburn, Pendine, Blackpool, Southport (50 miles), Lowestoft, Morecambe, Colwyn Bay, Lewes, Ramsgate, Brooklands Test Hill*, Ries Hill Climb, Edsvikens Ice Track, Syston, etc.

Southport—Standing mile, C. M. Needham, 1st. Flying kilo, C. M. Needham, 100·8 m.p.h. 50 miles Championship, C. M. Needham. Fastest bike *v.* fastest car, 1 mile, C. M. Needham.

Weiner Nieustadt—Flying kilo, G. Brough.

* Brooklands Test Hill—R. Russell Coe. 7·3 secs. 39·9 m.p.h. A new record.

1926

Rochdale Club meeting at Birkdale, 10-mile sidecar race—H. Hudson, 1st.

Southport Sands, 10-mile sidecar race—H. Hudson, 1st.

Stalybridge, solo — A. Greenwood, 1st. 77·7 m.p.h.; sidecar — A. Greenwood 1st. 56·6 m.p.h.

Pendine Sands—R. Thomas, 1st. 75·2 m.p.h.

Avus Record Berlin—Rudolf Arndt, 1st.

Geneva-Basle race—Blickensdorfer, f.t.d. solo; Staehlin, f.t.d. sidecar.

Colwyn Bay—A. Greenwood, 94·74 m.p.h.

                H. Hudson. Won Tornado Cup.

Pendine Sands, Welsh T.T.—T. Spann, 1st.

Championship of Ireland—R. Matthews, 69·5 m.p.h.

Doncaster—A. Greenwood, 100·0 m.p.h.

Magilligan Strand, solo—H. Matthews, 1st; sidecar—T. D. Boyle, 1st.

Lake Percolilli Carnival, 1 mile s.s.—H. Baker, 78·26; 1 mile f.s. 98·36; 5 miles s.s. 91·001; 5 miles f.s. 92·539.

Basle Race, solo—Blickensdorfer, 1st; sidecar—Staehlin, 1st.

Saltburn Sands—A. Greenwood, 105·52

Cambridge University Trials—R. C. Symondson Solo F.T.D. SS100

1927

Southport, novice race—J. O. Cunliffe.

Cambridge University Trials—L. Currie.

Nice Championship—M. Price, 127 k.p.h.

Colwyn Bay—A. Greenwood, 88·24 m.p.h. sidecar; 108·43 m.p.h. solo.

St Andrews, 20-mile race—R. J. Braid, 1st.

Allhang Riederberg Hill Climb, sidecar—E. Meyer, 1st;

                      solo novice, Muchta.

Saltburn Sands—A. Greenwood, 1st.

Doncaster, novices race—R. W. Storey, 20·6 secs.

Pendine, 19-mile race—T. Spann, 1st; 8-mile race—F. W. Dixon, 1st; sidecar 1-mile race—C. F. Edwards, 1st; Welsh T.T.—T. Spann, 1st. Fourth time running and so won the Trophy.

Stalybridge, novice race—J. O. Cunliffe, 1st.

Southport, 50-mile race—J. O. Cunliffe.

Madresfield Drive, sidecar—A. G. Greenwood, 1st.

Lowestoft, sidecar—E. C. E. Baragwanath, 1st.

Southport, C. F. Edwards, 86·03 m.p.h., 1st; novice race—J. H. Carr, 76·61 m.p.h., 1st.

Arpajon, one-way kilometre—F. W. Dixon, 130 m.p.h.

Salzburg G.P.—E. Meyer, 1st.

Cefnsidan Sands—R. E. Thomas 2½-mile race solo, 1st; 10 miles solo, 25 miles solo and 50 miles solo 1st. All unlimited.

1928

Southport, straight mile—C. F. Edwards, 1st.

Doncaster, unlimited, George Brough, sidecar, 21·8 secs., 83·33 m.p.h.; L. Currie, solo, 19·2 secs., 93·75 m.p.h.

Madresfield—L. Currie, A.J.S. and Bleckley Cups for best time: 26·4 secs., 84·73 m.p.h.

Saltburn Sands, kilometre—R. W. Storey, 1st, 18·2 secs., 122·09 m.p.h.; George Brough, 2nd, 18·4 secs., 121·9 m.p.h.; J. H. Carr, 3rd, 106·52 m.p.h.

Carr won also the 3-, 4- and 20-mile amateur races.

Southport, 1-mile novice race—J. O. Cunliffe.

Pendine, unlimited—George Brough, 1st and f.t.d.

Altogether in 1928 G.B. won five 'finals', one at Pendine and four at Doncaster (14 July), and made fastest in the world, one-way kilo, at 130·6 at Arpajon.

1929

Southport, straight mile—C. F. Edwards, 1st; 10 miles sidecar—C. F. Edwards, 1st.

Furness Club Meeting—J. H. Carr, 1st.

Budapest, solo—E. Meyer, 115; sidecar—E. Meyer, 98.

Wallasey, 25-mile sidecar race—K. Sauer, 1st.

Saltburn Sands, flying kilo—R. W. Storey, 100·76 m.p.h.; one mile—R. W. Storey, 81·82 m.p.h.

Madresfield Drive, solo—R. W. Storey, 1st, 84·73 m.p.h.; sidecar—R. W. Storey, 1st, 79·89 m.p.h.

Pendine, 1-mile sprint—R. W. Storey, 1st; 10-mile race—J. H. Carr, 1st; 50-mile race—R. E. Thomas, 1st; 20-mile sidecar race—C. F. Edwards, 1st.

Arpajon—H. Le Vack, 129·05 m.p.h. World's then maximum.

1930

Southport, straight mile—C. F. Edwards, 1st, sidecar; 10-mile race— N. H. Buckley, 2nd, sidecar.

Arpajon, flying kilo—H. Le Vack, 129·061 m.p.h. World's then maximum; flying mile— H. Le Vack, 128·226 m.p.h.

Saltburn—50-mile race, J. H. Carr 1st, 66·8 m.p.h., a record.

Ingoldstadt, Bavaria, sidecar race—E. Meyer, 1st, 113·98 m.p.h., a record.

Southport (October), kilo f/s—J. H. Carr, 108·59 m.p.h.; mile f/s— J. H. Carr; Fastest bike *v.* fastest car—J. H. Carr.

1931

Southport, 100-mile race—J. H. Carr, 73·47 m.p.h.

Saltburn, flying kilo—R. W. Storey, 110·74 m.p.h.; one mile—R. W. Storey.

Pendine, Welsh T.T.—J. H. Carr; 50-mile race—J. H. Carr; 100-mile race.

Southport (August), 1 mile f/s—J. H. Carr; 25-mile race—J. H. Carr, 1st.

Gatwick, ¼-mile rolling start—C. R. Hobbs, 1st, 66·18 m.p.h. on *Moby Dick*; ¼ mile rolling start, sidecar—C. R. Hobbs, 1st, 59·21 m.p.h. on *Moby Dick*.

1932

Southport, kilo—J. H. Carr, 110·74 m.p.h.; 1 mile, 10 miles and 50 miles (all unlimited)—J. H. Carr; two fastest bikes *v.* two fastest cars—J. H. Carr.

Brighton, standing ½-mile, clutch start—R. W. Storey, 81·08 m.p.h., f.t.d., beating all cars; standing ½-mile, push start—E. C. E. Baragwanath, sidecar, 66·57 m.p.h.; standing ½-mile, push start—R. W. Storey, solo, 72·58 m.p.h. Fine conditions.

1933

Southport, straight mile—J. H. Carr, solo; 5 miles—J. H. Carr, solo; 11 miles—J. H. Carr, solo; 25 miles—J. H. Carr, solo.

Brighton, standing ½-mile, push start—R. W. Storey, 77·59 m.p.h. Wet conditions.

Southport, straight mile—J. H. Carr, solo; 5 miles—J. H. Carr, solo.

1934

Southport, 100-mile race and 100 guineas—J. H. Carr, 71·09 m.p.h.

Gatwick, ¼-mile rolling start—N. B. Pope, 56·55 m.p.h., f.t.d.

Brighton—N. B. Pope, 80·36 m.p.h., supercharged solo.

1935

Sellick's Beach, Australia, 5-mile championships—George Marques, 67·41 m.p.h.; 10-mile championships—George Marques, 67·6 m.p.h.

Syston, Inter-Varsity Speed Trials, ½-mile uphill—R. Laird (1,100 c.c.), solo, 58·15 m.p.h.; racing unlimited—E. C. Fernihough, solo, 58·82 m.p.h.; racing unlimited—E. C. Fernihough, sidecar, 57·58 m.p.h.

Gatwick, sidecar race—E. C. Fernihough, 14·33 secs.; unlimited solo— E. C. Fernihough, 11·72 secs.

Donington, sidecar race, 10 laps—K. Collett, 57·27 m.p.h.

Gatwick (August), sidecar race—E. C. Fernihough, 61·5 m.p.h.; solo race—E. C. Fernihough, 71·75 m.p.h.; six fastest riders' event— E. C. Fernihough, 70·34 m.p.h.

Brighton, unlimited solo—E. C. Fernihough, 87·38 m.p.h.; unlimited sidecar—E. C. Fernihough, 75·0 m.p.h.; fastest bike *v.* fastest car— E. C. Fernihough, 88·7 m.p.h. (car 79·36).

Southport—N. B. Pope, 107·55 m.p.h. (supercharged), f.t.d.
Syston, Cambridge Inter-Varsity Speed Trials—E. Fernihough, f.t.d.
  sidecar.

1936

Wallasey, 5-lap sand race, unlimited—B. Berry; 1 kilo—B. Berry.
Gatwick, unlimited—E. C. Fernihough, 78·0 m.p.h.
Brighton—E. C. Fernihough, 90·0 m.p.h., a record.

1937

Gatwick, unlimited—N. B. Pope, 12·19 secs. Six fastest event—N. B.
  Pope, 12·01 secs., f.t.d.

1938

Brooklands, kilo—E. C. Fernihough, 143·39 m.p.h.

1939

Cambridge Inter-Varsity Speed Trials, ½-mile—M. N. Mavrogordato,
  67 m.p.h.; s.s. 26·85 secs., f.t.d.
Gatwick, Bickell Trophy, s.s. ¼-mile—N. B. Pope, 11·53 secs.
Brooklands (July)—N. B. Pope, lap record 124·51 m.p.h. Remains for all
  time.

1947

Saltburn Sands, straight mile—R. Berry, 81·81 m.p.h.; flying mile—
  R. Berry, 124·5 m.p.h.
Hartlepool Promenade, unlimited ¼-mile—R. Berry, 14·2 secs., f.t.d.
Brighton, kilo—R. Berry, 25·96 secs., 86·17 m.p.h.

1948

Hartlepool—R. Berry, 13·8 secs. Course record.

1960—Witchford, Vintage mile—J. O. Cunliffe (1926 SS100), 41·65 secs.

Post-First War History of the Motor-Cycle Maximum World Record

SOLO MACHINES Flying Kilometre				secs.	m.p.h.
6. 7.24	Arpajon	H. Le Vack	Brough S-J.A.P.	18·79	119·0
5. 9.26	Arpajon	C. F. Temple	O.E.C.-Temple	18·43	121·4
25. 8.28	Arpajon	O. M. Baldwin	Zenith-J.A.P.	17·95	124·6
25. 8.29	Arpajon	H. Le Vack	Brough S-J.A.P.	17·33	129·1
24. 8.30	Arpajon	J. S. Wright	O.E.C.-J.A.P.	16·63	134·5
31. 8.30	Arpajon	J. S. Wright	O.E.C. Temple-J.A.P.	16·29	137·3
20. 9.30	Ingoldstadt	E. Henne	B.M.W.	16·25	137·7
6.11.30	Cork	J. S. Wright	Zenith-J.A.P.	14·84	151
3.11.32	Tat	E. Henne	B.M.W.	14·73	152
28.10.34	Gyon	E. Henne	B.M.W.	14·63	153
27. 9.35	Frankfurt	E. Henne	B.M.W.	14·06	159·1
12.10.35	Frankfurt	E. Henne	B.M.W.	13·235	169
19. 4.37	Gyon	E. Fernihough	Brough S-J.A.P.	13·175	169·8
5. 9.62	Utah	W. Johnson	Triumph		224·6
Flying Mile					
6. 7.24	Arpajon	H. Le Vack	Brough S-J.A.P.	30·27	118·9
5. 9.26	Arpajon	C. F. Temple	O.E.C.-Temple	29·88	120·5
25. 8.28	Arpajon	O. M. Baldwin	Zenith-J.A.P.	28·92	124·5
25. 8.29	Arpajon	H. Le Vack	Brough S-J.A.P.	28·5	128·3
31. 8.30	Arpajon	J. S. Wright	O.E.C. Temple-J.A.P.	26·5	135·8
20. 9.30	Ingoldstadt	E. Henne	B.M.W.	26·39	136·5
11. 5.31	Neunkirchner	E. Henne	B.M.W.	24·73	145·5
3.11.32	Tat	E. Henne	B.M.W.	24·44	147·3
28.10.34	Gyon	E. Henne	B.M.W.	23·55	152·8
27. 9.35	Frankfurt	E. Henne	B.M.W.	22·915	157·1
12.10.36	Frankfurt	E. Henne	B.M.W.	22·050	163·2
7.11.36	Gyon	E. Fernihough	Brough S-J.A.P.	21·975	163·8
19. 4.37	Gyon	E. Fernihough	Brough S-J.A.P.	21·38	168·4
11.37	Frankfurt	E. Henne	B.M.W. S./chgd.		173·67
4.51	Ingoldstadt	W. Herz	N.S.U. S/chgd.		180·17
SIDECAR MACHINES Flying Kilometre					
6. 7.24	Arpajon	H. Le Vack	Brough S-J.A.P.	22·42	99·8
5. 9.26	Arpajon	C. F. Temple	O.E.C.-Temple	21·49	104·1
6. 2.29	Sweden	E. Magner	Royal Enfield-J.A.P.	20·23	110·6
8. 3.30	Sweden	E. Magner	Royal Enfield-J.A.P.	19·69	113·7
9. 3.30	Sweden	E. Magner	Royal Enfield-J.A.P.	19·045	117·5
19. 4.31	Neunkirchner	E. Henne	B.M.W.	18·865	118·6
30. 4.32	Tat	Alan Bruce	Brough S-J.A.P.	17·98	124·3
28.10.34	Gyon	E. Henne	B.M.W.	17·33	129·1
19. 4.37	Gyon	E. Fernihough	Brough S-J.A.P.	16·315	137·1
Flying Mile					
6. 7.24	Arpajon	H. Le Vack	Brough S-J.A.P.	36·10	99·7
5. 9.26	Arpajon	C. F. Temple	O.E.C.-Temple	34·8	103·5
25. 8.29	Arpajon	J. S. Wright	Zenith-J.A.P.	34·53	104·3
8. 3.30	Sweden	E. Magner	Royal Enfield-J.A.P.	31·37	114·7*
9. 3.30	Sweden	E. Magner	Royal Enfield-J.A.P.	30·57	117·7*
19. 4.31	Neunkirchner	E. Henne	B.M.W.	30·45	118·2
30. 4.32	Tat	Alan Bruce	Brough S-J.A.P.	29·235	123·1
28.10.34	Gyon	E. Henne	B.M.W.	27·94	128·8
19. 4.37	Gyon	E. Fernihough	Brough S-J.A.P.	26·635	135·2

* Note faster than the kilometre.
The above covers reciprocating engines only.

APPENDIX G

INSTRUCTION BOOK

Late edition, brown cover, 5⅝ in. by 3⅞ in.

FOREWORD

1—I appreciate that the great majority of 'Brough Superior' riders are experienced motor cyclists, therefore this booklet is by no means comprehensive, but is only intended to enlighten the rider on certain adjustments and hints peculiar to 'Brough Superior' motor cycles. I take a particular pride in my After Sales Service, and am always pleased to hear from riders of my machines, therefore, should any further information be required than is contained in this book, do not hesitate, to write to me direct.

In all correspondence, please make a particular note to include
ENGINE AND FRAME NUMBERS AND YEAR OF MACHINE.

The Engine number will be found stamped on the top of the Timing Chest, and the Frame number on the Front of Headlug near the bottom.

The above is particularly important when spare parts are ordered, and wherever possible I advise that pattern parts also be sent along.

(facsimile signature) GEORGE BROUGH.

ENGINE

2—Running in. It is particularly important that speeds exceeding 40 m.p.h. solo, and 35 m.p.h. sidecar, should not be indulged in until machine has done 500 miles. Maximum speeds may be increased up to a further 10 m.p.h. until the 1,000 mark has been reached. The first decarbonisation is recommended when the machine has done 1,500 miles, and prolonged all out speeds should not be maintained until the engine has been decarbonised and the high spots removed. The performance of engine will then well repay the above instructions being rigidly adhered to.

3—Dry Sump Models. After the first 500 miles and whilst the engine is warm drain the oil by taking off the two oil pipes and screwing out the Oil Union with Filter Gauze (this is the one nearest the chain side of machine). Clean out tank with paraffin and thoroughly drain. Clean Filter and replace. Refit oil pipes at the tank end and fill up with good clean oil (see Oil Recommendation). Leave the oil pipes off the pump end until the oil runs through and then connect up. Start up engine and ascertain that the oil is returning to the tank correctly (this is to ensure that no air-lock has taken place in the above procedure). It is recommended that the above operation of changing oil be carried out again at the first decarbonisation, and afterwards every 1,000 miles. Always keep plenty of oil in the tank. It is advisable to occasionally look into the tank after starting up to verify that the oil is returning, because an air leak in the system will upset the lubrication arrangements. Underneath the pump will be found a large knurled adjusting knob, this regulates the flow of oil to the hottest part of the front cylinder. This adjuster should not be touched unless trouble is experienced with oiling up of plugs in which case screw out one notch.

4—Mechanical Pump Models. This pump is set slightly on the liberal side when originally turned out from the works, and unless trouble is experienced with the oiling up of plugs, do not interfere with the setting until after decarbonisation, when it may be reduced slightly. The correct setting is pump delivering 20 drops per minute at engine revs. approximating 20 m.p.h. For heavy going, or continual high speed work it is advisable to make use of the extra oil pump by means of the control affixed to the handlebars. Should trouble be caused by over-oiling and continual oiling up of plugs, for no apparent reason, it is advisable to remove the Oil Pipe leading to the front cylinder from the oil tank, let the machine stand for a time and ascertain whether oil is leaking past the Ball Valve at the bottom of the extra oil pump; if so, remove the valve complete and thoroughly wash in paraffin, refit and test before connecting up again. A small particle of foreign matter from the tank might prevent the ball from seating properly, thus allowing extra oil to get into the engine with the resultant over-oiling mentioned above.

5—Starting Hints. When cold always flood the carburettor until it runs over. Open throttle about $\frac{2}{3}$, air closed, and give 4 or 5 kicks over with the valves lifted. If machine has been standing for any considerable time, or climatic conditions are extremely severe, it will be found on 11–50 models that by covering up $\frac{7}{8}$ of the air aperture of the carburettor, either by hand or a flat piece of cardboard with holes pierced, this will help the starting considerably (whatever is used, must be immediately removed when the engine fires). Now set throttle so that it is only very slightly open (because the smaller the opening the greater the suction in the inlet pipe), ignition about $\frac{2}{3}$ advanced, press kick-starter pedal down until the compression stroke is reached, lift valves and only slightly press down to pass the T.D.C. position; now release valve lifter and let kick-starter return to normal position. Give the kick-starter a good hefty swing which will bounce over the next compression stroke, and usually results in the engine starting up immediately. This method of starting up by bouncing over compression is soon acquired by practice and will be found very effective.

6—Tappet Adjustment. On the side-valve models, this should always be carried out when the engine is *hot*, and the correct setting is ·003″ inlet and ·005″ exhaust. Overhead-valve models should be set when cold so that the valve stem end cap is just free to revolve, i.e., with no up and down movement at all.

7—Sparking Plugs. K.L.G., K7 plugs on 11–50 models, and K.L.G., K1 on all other models are originally fitted. These should be cleaned at frequent intervals, and two of the three points set at ·018″, the other ·022″.

8—Engine (General). Cylinder head bolts should always be kept well tightened down, and should be checked over occasionally with the special spanner provided in the tool kit. A little oil brushed on to the valves and springs on overhead valve models occasionally is advised.

9—Decarbonising. In addition to removing the obvious items such as exhaust and inlet pipes, etc., it is advisable to take off the tank as this makes the head bolts easily accessible. Remove front head, barrel and piston first, cover over crankcase, and remove rear cylinder head. Get piston at the bottom of the stroke, raise the barrel as high as possible, remove gudgeon pin circlip (care should be taken to cover the crankcase in case this is dropped) push out gudgeon pin, slide piston up the barrel, and then remove. The rear barrel cannot be removed unless this procedure is carried out. When reassembling the engine, reverse this order, completing the assembly of piston and barrel of rear cylinder before working on the front. Clean the faces of cylinder barrels and head by lapping with fine grinding paste on a sheet of glass or any dead flat surface. Assemble with a smearing of good jointing compound on both barrel and head before inserting gasket, also put a little graphite on the threads of holding down bolts and tighten down evenly all round. When engine has been run for a short time again tighten down these bolts.

Important. Arrange that all parts removed from the engine such as gudgeon pins, pistons, valves etc., be marked in such a manner to ensure that they are assembled in their original positions i.e., pistons and gudgeons might be marked on the timing side, say one mark for the rear and two for the front, and valves 1, 2, 3 and 4, counting from the rear of engine. In reassembling engine be sure and smear all working surfaces with clean oil. Whenever valve circlips are removed, it will be necessary to fit new ones; be sure and have a few by you! Piston ring gaps should be ·004″.

10—Carburettor (adjustments on '11–50' Twin Carburettor Models). It is imperative that the adjustment of *both* throttle slides should be synchronous. This is best affected by tuning the front and the back cylinders as two separate engines, e.g., supposing the engine has been dismantled and re-assembled, and both carburettors fitted up, remove rear sparking plug, start up the front engine, allow it to warm up, then adjust the small bolt which controls the shut-off position of the throttle slide, at the same time varying the adjustment of the Pilot Jet until the engine is ticking over as slowly as possible. The cable adjusting screw at the top of the carburettor should be adjusted so that there is the slightest amount of movement on the control grip before the wire actually begins to lift the throttle slide. Now repeat this procedure with the rear cylinder and with the front plug removed.

11—Forks (Castle). The most important item is the constant lubrication of the bottom fork link spindle, and shock absorber rod ends (greasers are provided on all points). Lubricate the long springs running inside the front spring tubes by squirting oil through the side slots. Should play develop in the bottom pins this can be taken up by removing the outside plain washer, and fitting a thicker one. Up and down play on these pins can only be remedied by fitting new pins and bushes. Occasionally remove both shock absorbers complete and smear graphite on the shock absorber centre body on the fork. Shock absorber adjustment should be such that when forks are pressed down they only slowly return to their normal position by the spring tension.

12—Monarch (bottom link pattern). Constant lubrication to the bottom link spindle is very important to retain the sweet action of the fork. To take up play in the centre links, loosen all four nuts, slacken shock absorbers right back, turn each spindle a little at a time by means of the square end, in a clock-wise direction; leave a little play as this is usually taken up when the four nuts are tightened.

13—Steering Head. Place the machine so that the front wheel is clear of the ground. (Castle) Tighten up the lower of the two Ring nuts under the handlebar lug, ascertain that play has been taken up, then lock up with smaller ring nut. (Monarch) Slacken off the bolt that goes across the fork girder, also the short one that grips the steering column, then tighten down by means of the large Hexagon nut. Be sure that all bolts and nuts are tightened down after adjusting. Adjust head on the tight side for side-car work.

14—Chains. When originally turned out, the primary chain is riveted up; cranked links are not fitted to this chain, and under no circumstances should these be fitted. The primary chain runs in an oil bath and provides a positive form of lubrication to the chain. Remove the level plug near the bottom of case, fill up with oil, via the inspection disc until it runs out at the plug hole. Under no circumstances fill up higher than this plug level. This should be carried out with the machine off the stand.

15—Chain Adjustment (Primary). Slacken the $\frac{5}{8}''$ bolt securing the top of gear box to frame, but do not disturb the pin securing bottom of gear box to frame as the gear box is free to pivot on this pin. Take up play by means of the special adjuster. The correct adjustment should not be more than $\frac{1}{2}''$ up and down play at the tightest point. (Rear) Slacken rear wheel spindle nuts and then tighten by means of the adjusters on the frame fork ends, giving one half turn to each bolt.

16—Gear Box. When originally turned out, the gear box contains a mixture of 50/50 Speedwell Crimsangere and engine oil, and is filled up to the filler level plug on the box cover. After the first 500 miles check and replenish, afterwards every 1,000 miles. It is advisable to keep the box slightly over-lubricated as any excess works its way out on to the rear chain.

17—Clutch Wire. The clutch wire should be adjusted to allow $\frac{1}{16}''$ play on the clutch lever on the handlebars.

18—Gear Adjustment. If tank is removed for any reason, the gears should be checked over and if necessary re-adjusted (this only applies to hand change gears). It will be noticed that a spring plunger in box locates the actual gear, and it is advisable to set the small operating arm of the side of the box in the second and third gear positions respectively and check these over on the tank gate. Any discrepancy can be taken up by means of the adjustable yokes on the gear rods. If this is done the top and bottom gears will automatically be correct.

19—Gear Changing. When changing up do not shut off but keep the engine turning over fairly fast (especially in the lower gears and whilst machine is new) then snap the gear through sharply—do not attempt to slide the gears through. Make good use of the third gear as this is fairly high and is very useful when overtaking. Keep all yokes and pins regularly oiled.

20—Wheels (Lubrication of Bearings). Journal ball bearings are fitted and are non-adjustable. Bearings are packed with grease when originally turned out; it is advisable to repack with grease every 6,000 miles.

21—Front Wheel and Brake. To remove front wheel, remove brake tackle and knock out spindle, let wheel drop, push over sideways so as to slide the shackle arm off the pin on forks. Should difficulty be experienced in removing brake anchor plate owing to the nut on the opposite side un-screwing, tighten this up dead tight, and hold wheel in vice by means of the large hexagon nut on the side opposite to the brake, then place a spanner on the nut on brake side, and *tap sharply* in an anti-clockwise direction. Should the front Anchor plate rattle, remove the large star washer and set the points so that more tension is put on the plate. When refitting this star washer be sure and see that it fits over the projecting end of floating bush, and is not trapped between the nut and the bush end. Occasionally put a drop of oil on the front brake floating bush, this is situated right in the centre of the brake anchor plate. Keep the shackle arm securing the brake anchor plate to forks well lubricated.

22—Rear Wheel. To remove rear wheel take off the detachable portion of the rear mudguard, slacken spindle nuts, remove anchor plate bolt, speedometer cable from angle drive, rear brake rod adjuster and chain, and slide wheel out. Check for alignment when re-fitting. Occasionally check over the three sprocket retaining nuts and put a little oil between the outside retaining ring and sprocket.

QUICKLY DETACHABLE AND INTERCHANGEABLE WHEELS

23—Rear Wheel. After removing the rear split portion of guard, withdraw the long knockout spindle thus allowing the large packing piece to drop out. This enables the wheel to slide off the three pegs on the rear of brake drum and drop out. This operation should not take more than a few seconds.

To Replace Wheel. Lift wheel into position and then push knockout spindle straight through. This will carry the weight of the wheel. Now position the wheel on to the three driving pegs, insert packing piece as far as it will go. Withdraw knockout spindle (driving pegs will hold wheel in position) push packing piece into correct position, now re-insert knockout spindle and tighten up wheel.

Front Wheel. Remove the brake wire, withdraw knockout spindle, move the wheel over slightly which will enable the brake shackle to slide off the securing pin and drop out.

To Interchange the Wheels. After both have been removed from the frame remove the lock rings (left-hand thread rear wheel, right-hand thread front wheel) when the innards of each can be taken out and re-fitted in to the required wheel.

24—Spring Frame. To correctly adjust the spring frame, jack the machine up in the region of the gear box, allowing the rear wheel to stand clear of the ground. To take up play in the stabiliser assembly, slacken off all four rocker bar nuts, also shock absorber nuts, turn spindles by means of the square ends in an anti-clockwise direction. Do not take up play completely as a little is taken up when the end nuts are tightened. Adjust one spindle, tighten up end nuts, and check up and down movement before adjusting the other spindle. Adjust shock absorber nuts equally on both sides so that when rear portion of frame is lifted it will only slowly return to its former position. Rear fork and shock absorbers may be screwed up dead tight. Main rocker bar through frame requires no adjustment, but regular greasing is essential; grease remainder of spring frame where nipples are provided, once a week.

24a—Tyre Pressures.

	Front	Rear
Overhead 680 Rigid Frame	22 lbs.	18 lbs.
'11–50'	24 lbs.	20 lbs.
'SS100'	25 lbs.	22 lbs.
'SS80'	25 lbs.	20 lbs.
Black Alpine 680 Spring Frame	24 lbs.	22 lbs.
'11–50' Spring Frame	24 lbs.	22 lbs.
'SS100' Spring Frame	25 lbs.	22 lbs.

The above pressures are for solo riding. When side-car is attached, increase pressures by 3 lbs. per tyre. Side-car tyres $27 \times 4 \cdot 00$ require 19 lbs., and $26 \times 3 \cdot 50$, 21 lbs., for the standard 'Cruiser' 21 lbs., for large touring and two-seater side-cars increase pressures 3 lbs.

LIGHTING SET

25—Battery. Maintain acid level about $\frac{1}{4}''$ above the plates by adding distilled water fortnightly. Keep terminals clean and smeared with petroleum jelly. Check voltage when filling up and if same is below minimum specified by makers have same re-charged from a separate source.

26—Magdyno. Check contact breaker points and reset to gauge on mag spanner, and clean points if pitted or dirty. See that cam-ring revolves freely in its housing and smear outer surface of same with oil about every 1,000 miles. Keep high-tension leads clear of hot or moving parts, check cut-out points, clean if necessary, but do not alter setting. All brushes should be kept free in their holders and commutator and pick-up ring surfaces clean.

27—Dynamo Charging. In the event of the dynamo failing to show a charge on the Ammeter, remove dynamo end cap and examine the control brush which is the bottom brush on the dynamo. This trouble is usually caused by the tension of the spring on the brush being insufficient to enable it to make good contact with the commutator. To rectify, set the spring arm closer to the brush.

28—Wiring. It is important that all earth connections be kept clean and tight and all wires away from moving parts.

GENERAL

29—Clean out petrol tap, pipes and filter at botton of carburettor every 1,000 miles whilst machine is comparatively new. Petrol taps are fitted with filters inside the tank.

30—Oil recommended is Speedwell Sans Egal for touring and Speedwell White Ideal for racing. Where these are unobtainable use only first-class oils in sealed tins.

31—Keep the small vent holes in petrol and oil tank filler caps quite clear to prevent air lock. Add an eggcupful of oil to each tank of petrol, particularly whilst the machine is new.

32—Magneto Timing should be contact breaker points breaking $\frac{9}{16}$″ before T.D.C. with magneto full advanced, excepting SS100 and Overhead 680 which should be $\frac{11}{16}$″.

33—Twist Grips. Do not allow the mag. twist grip to retard whilst riding because apart from the lack of performance it will cause discoloration of the exhaust pipes. The ignition twist grip should always be kept on the tight side to prevent the possibility of retarding without the driver noticing it. Should the twist grips work too freely they may be damped slightly by screwing in the small grub screw in the plated ring at the end of the rubber grip.

34—Fuel. Always run on Ethyl, B.P. Plus or a No. 1 grade of petrol.

35—Controls. All controls open (or advance) inwards towards the rider. The knurled ebonite ring on the left handlebar operates the dipping beam of headlamp.

Excerpts from the earlier Instruction Book, grey cover $7\frac{1}{8}″ \times 4\frac{5}{8}″$:

NOTE FROM THE MANUFACTURER. There is nothing gives me more satis faction than to see one of my productions properly cared for. After all, you have paid a high price for a high class article and it is only reasonable that I should request you, in your own interests, and that of the machine that bears my name, to give the essential details of the machine the requisite amount of attention periodically. I am a hard rider myself and I appreciate that half-an-hour a week spent in checking the adjustment and lubrication of wheels, chains, tappets, steering head and gear box will be amply repaid by the continued hard service with absence of trouble the machine will give. I am at all times very pleased to hear from Brough Superior riders on any point with which they may be in difficulty.

GEORGE BROUGH.

TOE OPERATED BRAKE. As the leverage obtained by this lever is very considerable, pressure should be applied lightly at first until the necessary pressure to be applied is found.

MAGDYNO. When Magdyno, as fitted to a solo machine, is required to light a sidecar lamp, additional to those on the machine, a large battery should be substituted, if much night riding is to be undertaken. Machines supplied from the Works for use with sidecar are fitted with the necessary large battery.

TYRES AND TYRE PRESSURES. For general solo riding, the front tyre should be pumped hard and the rear tyre medium, according to the load each tyre has to carry. For sidecar use all tyres should be pumped fairly hard, and the sidecar tyre quite hard. Correct inflation has a very important bearing on the life of a tyre and maintenance of full pressure lessens deterioration. Rim dents and rims running out of truth can only lead to tyre trouble, therefore remove these faults as soon as possible.

PACKING TOOLS. The tool roll should have a piece of rag laid on the tools before rolling up, and the strap done up as tight as possible. Loose tools, etc., should be wrapped tight and packed tight.

GAS GENERATORS. These must be kept very clean, if trouble is to be avoided. Re-charge generator every time lamp is used. Whilst doing this blow through gas passage. Renew gas filter every 100 hours of lighting. Keep water container empty until some little time before it is required, and on filling prove free flow of water. Blow through gas tube, and *turn on water only to usual position for full flame*, and wait for gas to generate. A gas bag will avoid many troubles. If burner becomes choked, renew the burner.

Specification of the Motor-Car—$3\frac{1}{2}$ Litres

ENGINE—6 cylinders in line, side by side valves, bore 76·2 mm., stroke 127 mm. Lanchester vibration damper at forward end.

CARBURETTOR—Downdraught; with automatic choke control, giving easy starting and automatic mixture regulation throughout the entire temperature range.

TRANSMISSION—Synchro-shift gear box with remote control. Three speeds forward and reverse.

CLUTCH—Oil-cushioned single-plate type, with heat-treated cork inserts.

REAR AXLE—Semi-floating. Spiral bevel drive.

FUEL SYSTEM—12-gallon tank at rear. Two-level tap. Engine-driven fuel pump.

COOLING SYSTEM—Specially designed radiator, with unusually large radiating surface. Unique type fan ensuring a maximum temperature of 86°C. under any conditions. Passenger's compartment completely insulated by special type bulkhead. Special louvres to relieve pressure under bonnet.

CHASSIS—Box-girder type, with double 'X' member in centre. Strongly braced throughout.

SUSPENSION—Special long semi-elliptic springs front and rear, Oversize slow-moving Luvax shock-absorbers front and back. Covers on all springs.

WHEELS—$16 \times 6 \cdot 00$ inches. Fitted Goodyear 'G3' tyres. All wheels, including spare, have specially designed Ace-avion discs. Spare wheel fitted Ace cover. Wheelbase—10 feet. Track—4 feet $9\frac{1}{2}$ inches.

BRAKES—Duo-Automatic Hydraulic Brakes, that give double safe stopping with a separate safety braking system which takes hold automatically in emergencies.

STEERING GEAR—Worm selector type. Specially developed and suitably geared for high speed. The steering is of a new principle that enables the car to hold direction without swerving or 'wandering'; unaffected by spring action, braking or road conditions.

JACKING SYSTEM—Four hydraulic jacks, operated from driver's seat. Control valve permits front, or rear, or all four wheels to be raised at a time. Car can be raised in two minutes and lowered in five seconds.

AUTOMATIC CHASSIS LUBRICATION—All moving parts of chassis lubricated from a reservoir, by engine suction.

ELECTRICAL EQUIPMENT—Twelve-volt (automatic voltage control) generator and starter are fitted. Cut-out, junction box, trafficator fuse and horn relay conveniently placed under bonnet.

LIGHTING—Two P170 Lucas headlamps, two wing lamps, rear lamp, combined stop and reversing light (latter operated automatically by gear lever), interior lights in roof and diffused dashboard lights.

INSTRUMENTS—Mounted on handsome walnut facia board. All dials visible to the driver. Speedometer—5-inch, reading to 100 m.p.h. Ammeter. Water Thermometer. Oil Level Tell-tale. Petrol gauge. Switches for Dashboard and Roof. Lamps. Engine Starting Switch, Head and Side Lamp Switch.

EQUIPMENT—Special Lucas synchronised Wind Horns. Flush-mounted Trafficators. Combined Clock and Driving Mirror. Hidden Master Switch. Twin Windscreen Wipers, interconnected. Aluminium Number Plates and Licence Holder. Complete Kit of Tools, Spare Fuses, etc. Specially designed Bumpers. Wing Mirror. Two-level Petrol Tap.

LUGGAGE ACCOMMODATION—Of ample dimensions to take four full-size suitcases and number of smaller packages.

SPEED—85 m.p.h.

PETROL CONSUMPTION—20 to 22 m.p.g.

APPENDIX I

Miscellaneous Notes

The 'SS80–100'—During 1926 Haydn Road listed what the maker called the 'SS80–100' having a similar specification to the SS80 already noted but with a modified engine giving road speeds in excess of the usual 80 m.p.h. The engine although of standard dimensions, viz. 85·5 × 86 m/m 988 c.c. had four cams of similar profile to those used in the SS100 A.G.S. of this year. The ports were highly polished, there were roller bearings to the big-ends and main shaft and all valves were of chrome-vanadium steel. Each exhaust pipe had an aluminium heat dissipator close to the port identical to that for the front cylinder shown in Fig. 22. The remainder of the bicycle followed standard SS80 practice except that Castle forks were included in the list price of £150 for the solo magneto model and £160 for the solo magdyno model.

It is recorded that twenty-two such specials were made and probably a further eight. Several went to Japan.

M.A.G. engines—On the 748 c.c. engine the forked rod was to the rear cylinder.

J.A.P. engines—On the 1921 '90 bore' engine the forked rod was to the front cylinder.

In the 4-cam engines release timing or rotary pump should occur when the rear inlet is just opening, the slot in the oil pump should be upright to the rear cylinder. The dot on the wheel to be in line with the R.H.S. of the slot when the wheel is in position.

The 8–45 h.p. engines have 68 big-end rollers and the big-end packing washers from the sprocket side are 1 thin, 1 thick, 1 thin, 1 thick and 1 thin.

Piston clearances for racing engines both 80 bore and square: top 20–25 thous. Bottom 12 thous. Fitting of valve guides on S.V. SS80's, top of guide to valve cap seating = 2″. The first 8–30 pistons were fitted with $\frac{3}{32}$″ rings in September 1928, i.e. for 1929 season and all these engines so fitted bear the symbol mark S, thus KTCY/S. Engines not so fitted should be marked F after the engine number thus, KTCY/C . . . F.

Valve clearance on racing engines, both square and long stroke. With piston at T.D.C. exhaust valve should have $\frac{5}{32}$″ to $\frac{3}{16}$″ of movement from the valve seating to top of piston. Compression ratios on 2 and 4 cam S.V. engines should be 5:1. C.C. at t.d.c. should be 112 to 117. $\frac{1}{32}$″ plate under cylinder of any 8 h.p. engine = 4 c.c. $\frac{1}{32}$″ off a valve cap = 3 c.c.

Rotary valves. Timing of rotary valves on 1930 8–50 engine. Valve should be open when rear cylinder is at b.d.c. On 8–30 and 8–50's prior to 1930, valve should close when front cylinder reaches b.d.c.

Trail on December 1930 A.G.S. spring frame with 27×4 rear wheel and 28×3.5 front wheel and standard Castle fork = 3″. Weight of December 1936 SS100 = 4 cwt. 1 qr. = 476 lbs.

Trail on 680 c.c. spring frame with 26×3.5 rear and 26×3.25 front and standard Castle fork with $\frac{3}{4}$″ packing on bottom of steering column = $3\frac{3}{4}$″. Weight of rear wheel complete with 26×3.5 tyre = 41 lbs. Spring frame 680 c.c. 1930:

Weight on front wheel	= 1 cwt. 2 qrs. 7 lbs.
Weight on rear wheel	= 2 cwt. 21 lbs.
	= 3 cwt. 3 qrs.
	= 420 lbs.

Rigid frame 680 c.c.:

Weight on front wheel	= 1 cwt. 2 qrs. 7 lbs.
Weight on rear wheel	= 1 cwt. 3 qrs. 14 lbs.
Total weight	= 3 cwt. 1 qr. 21 lbs.
	= 385 lbs.

Black Alpine 680 c.c. 16T engine sprocket, 34 clutch, 19 gearbox and 45 rear = 5, 6, 10·25 and 13·5:1. With 22, 42, 17 and 45 top = 5·05:1. 1928 680 c.c. engine. 19 rollers in big-end, $1\frac{1}{8}''$ long plus two packings.

E. Meyer's engine. With ordinary cams the timing was:

	Exh. opens before b.d.c.	*Exh. closes after* t.d.c.
Front cylinder	75°	23°
Inlet	27°	70°
Rear cylinder	67°	26°
Inlet	31°	80°
With racing cams:		
Front cylinder	75°	25°
Inlet	21°	55°
Rear cylinder:	73°	22°
Inlet	25°	60°

His racing engine was $\dfrac{\text{JTOR/I.}}{87971/*}$ Flats filed on piston tops to give $\frac{5}{32}''$ clearance for the valve. C.R. 10·57:1. Magneto timing = $\frac{7}{8}''$ b.t.d.c. When supercharge C.R. Front = 6·1:1. Rear 7·1:1. Blower gives 15 p.s.i. Choke $1\frac{1}{4}''$. Jet 1600.

J.A.P. engines 4 cam, 1932 marked GTCY/S. With detachable heads have front piston $\frac{1}{4}''$ longer than the rear. The difference is from gudgeon pin to bottom of skirt. They are the same from gudgeon pin to top of piston on back and front. Overall length of front piston = $3\frac{1}{4}''$. Overall length of rear piston = $3''$.

11–50 and Touring sidecar, total weight = 5 cwt. 3 qrs. 21 lbs.
= 665 lbs.

O.H.V. 680 engines with SN after the number have roller bearings on the gear side composed of 15–$\frac{1}{8}''$ dia. × $\frac{5}{8}''$ long rollers.

Matchless engines. 1936 onwards were 85·5 × 85·5 mm. Matchless s.v. engines have 56, $\frac{1}{4}'' \times \frac{1}{4}''$ rollers in the big-end and 42–$\frac{1}{4}'' \times \frac{1}{4}''$ in driving side bearing. Gear side is a plain bearing. All engines from No. 4630 had a new drive side bearing as per part No. 38/BS/E 30/A w.e.f. 6 September 1937. This brings the crankcase $\frac{1}{4}''$ wider than in previous engines. First engine through works thus was on 9 December 1937.

The Index